Pra … *Game*

"This book sh … ans! It provides
hope and prom … an emptiness and
striving, and the promise that if you do like the protagonist of this brilliant story does, you will find peace and freedom. It is rare that a novel can change your life. This one not only entertains, but carries the seeds of personal transformation. If you are a highlighter, get your pen ready. There is much here that you will want to remember."

— **Suzanne Giesemann,**
Spiritual teacher and author of *The Awakened Way*

"It is our destiny to Awaken. It will happen for us all, if even in the final moments of our life. Here, Lise Villeneuve offers a way in which it can happen now and not later, by illustrating the path itself, in story form. A beautiful way for the mind to imprint toward a greater way of creating a life we love, and a beautiful testament to how we are redefining what it means to be human. Thank you Lise, for this must-read brilliance.

— **Dr. Sue Morter,**
Author of #1 Best-Selling *The Energy Codes* & *The God Body* (2026)

"Humanity is in the midst of one of the most significant growth spurts we have ever experienced, a time when we are beginning to emerge from a deep sleep and claim who we truly are and what is really happening here. This brilliant and insightful book will open you to the shift that is happening in human consciousness and how you can be a part of it. For all of humanity, I thank you, Lise, for your contribution to the healing of our planet!"

— **Mary O'Malley,**
Awakening Mentor and Author of *What's in the Way IS the Way* & *The Joy of Being Fully Alive*

"Rarely does a story feel so real and carry such deep spiritual resonance. *Unplugging from the Game* is a beautiful reminder that joy, freedom, and inner peace aren't something we earn—they're who we already are, once we unplug from fear and remember the truth. This isn't just a novel—it's a loving nudge back to your radiant self.* "

— Marci Shimoff,
#1 New York Times bestselling author of *Happy for No Reason & Chicken Soup for the Woman's Soul*

"WOW. A gift! Sometimes tears start to flow...the writing is so descriptive and poetic. I can see the words like a movie. It reminds me of home with our Irish expressions. It's brilliant. The whole book is a lesson and if one can read carefully...the sky's the limit. It's very easy to read, meaning it flows so organically. The wisdom is subtle and brilliantly connects in a way that's not too heavy or complicated to understand. I hope this book will be added as a necessary curriculum for schools. Imagine a world where children learned this beautiful knowledge."

— Sheila Knott

"This book is very useful to help teenagers and adults recenter themselves into reality and truly take a pause from daily, hardcore life. While reading the book, I found that it helped me realize more strongly and truthfully that humans really do play two different roles. Initially, I didn't quite know what to expect from the book, but as it progressed, it became more and more clear that it was made to serve a good purpose: to aid individuals find inner peace and acknowledge the fact that we must take control of our lives if we want to succeed and feel good within. Overall, my experience with this book was very positive. I think it's a great way for teens and adults to help themselves feel better in many ways."

— CDT, 16 years old

UNPLUGGING FROM THE GAME

Remembering the Real You

by

Lise Villeneuve

Unplugging from the Game: Remembering the Real You

ISBN: 978-1-0695773-2-0

Published by Conscious Living Solutions

First Edition, July 2025

Printed in Canada

Cover and interior design by Lise Villeneuve

Dedication

Dedicated to my family—

Rob, Emma, and Theo.

May your days be filled with love,

your hearts with peace,

and your lives with joy, meaning, and fulfillment.

Unplugging from the Game

Remembering the Real You

Unplugging from the Game: Remembering the Real You

Table of Contents

A Note on the Music Behind the Words

As I wrote this book, one album played on repeat—Estas Tonne's *Internal Flight.*
It wasn't just background music. It was a companion. A current. A pulse.
Each note seemed to bypass the thinking mind and stir something ancient and alive within me.

His music is more than sound—it's frequency.
It lifts, it moves, it reveals.

Internal Flight holds a kind of energy that aligns perfectly with the journey this story invites you into, and **I encourage you to listen to it as you read.**

It's free on YouTube: https://www.youtube.com/watch?v=BF3wM5Onh6c

Let it breathe between the lines. Let it guide you inward. It might just elevate the way this story lands in your heart.

With deep gratitude to Estas Tonne,
for creating music that awakens the soul.

Author's Note

A Journey Back to the Real You

Hey there, fellow traveler—

I'm so glad you're here.

I wrote this story because I believe there's a powerful truth buried beneath everything we've been taught about who we are and how life works. It's not something we usually learn in school, or talk about in boardrooms or coffee shops. In fact, most people go their entire lives without discovering it. But once you catch even a glimpse—once you feel it—everything begins to shift.

For much of my life, I believed that success, achievement, and approval were the ultimate measures of worth. That stress and struggle were just part of the deal. That my thoughts were facts. That life was happening to me. I tried to manage and control everything—my work, my relationships, even my sense of self—without realizing the real journey wasn't external.

It was inward.

It wasn't until years later, after searching, stumbling, and experiencing more than a few wake-up calls, that I began to recognize the deeper patterns shaping my life. The programming. The invisible scripts. The generational conditioning that kept me looping through anxiety, performance, and self-doubt—without ever questioning why.

And I realized something simple but profound:

Growing up, nobody had ever handed me a guide for waking up.

That's why I wrote this book.

This isn't just Brayden's story—it's all of ours. A journey of remembering. Of unplugging from the noise, the pressure, and the unconscious patterns that keep us locked in survival mode and disconnected from our deeper wisdom. It's about seeing through the illusion and finally stepping into the life we were meant to live—one rooted in clarity, purpose, and peace.

This isn't about fixing yourself.

Because the truth is—you're not broken.

It's about reclaiming your power.

Returning to the truth of who you really are.

Here's what *Unplugging from the Game* will invite you to explore:

How to see through unconscious programming.
Understand the invisible beliefs and emotional patterns that keep you stuck—and how to move beyond them.

How to stop living from the mind alone.
Learn to shift from thought-based reactivity to embodied presence and intuitive awareness.

How to clear emotional and energetic blockages.
Discover how unprocessed emotions show up in your body—and how to release what no longer serves you.

How to live as an Energy Being, not just an identity.
Reconnect with your true nature: expansive, grounded, connected, and whole.

How to become the conscious creator of your reality.
Recognize the link between your beliefs, your energy, and your outcomes—and learn to lead your life from the inside out.

This is the path of remembrance.

Of peeling back the layers.

Of coming home to the clarity that's always been within you.

If something in Brayden's story stirred something in you—however subtle—I believe you found this book for a reason.

And maybe—just maybe—you're ready to unplug from the game too.

With warmth,

Lise Villeneuve

Chapter 1

Entering the Simulation

The Characters

Brayden couldn't breathe.

He gripped the edges of the bathroom sink, sweat beading along his temples, heart pounding like it was trying to punch its way out of his chest. Cold water ran uselessly from the tap as he stared into the mirror, trying to remember how to be a person.

What's wrong with me?

His vision shimmered. His fingers tingled. This wasn't nerves. This wasn't stress. This was panic.

A full-blown panic attack.

He had never had one before—at least, not that he'd recognized. And now, in the middle of his own surprise party, he couldn't even pull himself together long enough to unwrap a present.

Through the door, he could hear the laughter, the clinking glasses, the background hum of music and voices. His party. His people. His life.

You're fine, he told himself. *Smile. Breathe. Don't fall apart now.*

He straightened up, forced his jaw to unclench, and opened the door.

The moment he stepped out, the crowd burst into song.

"Happy birthday to you…"

He froze for half a second, then walked into the chorus of voices, balloons, and camera flashes like an actor hitting his mark. The house shimmered with celebration—golden streamers, floating numbers that read "50," wine in every hand, and faces beaming with love and champagne.

He gave them what they wanted. He clapped. He grinned. He laughed in the right places. But inside, the panic was still pulsing just beneath the surface.

What's wrong with me?

Holly was radiant, all red lipstick and joyful chaos. She rushed up, arms outstretched, and hugged him like they were the only two people in the room. "Happy birthday, sweetheart," she whispered.

The kids followed. Maggie, 18, glowing and self-assured, clapped with contagious enthusiasm. David, 16, already taller than Brayden, gave him a solid slap on the back, his brown curls bouncing. Lily, 13, hovered near the food table, carefully adjusting appetizer trays with quiet urgency, like each one had to be perfect or the night would collapse.

Then came Jake—hands in his pockets, grinning like he had personally orchestrated the whole event.

"Fifty," he said, shaking his head. "The man. The myth. The guy who still thinks the Oilers are gonna win the Cup."

Laughter rippled through the room. Jake raised his glass.

"To Brayden," he said. "Reliable as sunrise. Sharp as ever. Loyal to a fault. And the only person I know who's both a genius at work and completely unreachable after 9 p.m. You've built a beautiful life, man. And somehow, you've managed to stay sane through all of it. We love you, buddy."

Holly lifted her glass too. "To my husband—the calm in the storm, the rock, the heart of this family."

More applause. Glasses clinked. People smiled at him like he was everything they said he was.

Brayden raised his own glass. Smiled. Nodded.

But inside…

I should feel grateful. I should feel happy. I should feel sane.

He looked around the room at the people he loved. The people who loved him. And all he could feel was a disturbing restlessness inside.

He couldn't put it into words yet, but the idealized version of himself was no longer capable of hiding or silencing the one screaming underneath. His insecurities, his unease, the quiet shame he'd buried for years—were rising fast. Ignoring the pain was no longer an option. The mask was cracking, and the shadows he thought he'd sealed away were starting to spill out.

It was terrifying.

Holly handed him a gift—a sleek, beautifully wrapped box.

"Open it," she said, her eyes sparkling.

Brayden peeled the paper away. Inside was a black leather jacket. Silver zippers. Stitched detail. Soft as butter.

The room broke into cheers. Maggie squealed. David fist-pumped.

"Now you'll actually look cool on your Harley," David said.

"Try it on, Dad!" Maggie laughed.

He slipped the jacket on. It fit perfectly, hugging his broad shoulders like it was made for him.

But even wrapped in new leather, Brayden felt like a fraud.
Like someone wearing a costume for a role he wasn't sure he ever auditioned for.

The party buzzed around him. Music. Laughter. Posed photos. Warm lights. He nodded, shook hands, gave hugs. But his mind was drifting again—somewhere quieter. Somewhere lonelier.

Outside the window, dusk had settled over the trees. The sky was softening into night.

Then the lights dimmed, and Holly reappeared with a towering chocolate cake, candles glowing like tiny stars.

"Make a wish!" someone shouted, as the singing began again.

Brayden leaned in. The heat of the candles brushed his face. The smell of chocolate filled his lungs.

He closed his eyes.

And a thought rose—sharp and clear:

I just want to know what's missing.

He blew out the candles.

Applause erupted. People cheered. Someone popped more confetti.

Brayden opened his eyes, smiled on cue, and nodded.

But something had shifted.

He didn't know it yet, but the answer he was searching for wasn't in the cake, the jacket, or the applause. It wouldn't come from a gift or a conversation or even from Holly's eyes, filled with so much love.

It was already on its way.

That night—while the last guests trickled out, while the decorations sagged, while the dishwasher hummed and the lights were dimmed—something would happen.

Not through a person.

Not through a moment.

But through a dream that would pull back the veil and reveal everything he'd spent a lifetime forgetting.

The real game was about to begin. And it would change everything.

The Lucid Dream

Brayden lay in bed, staring at the ceiling as the last echoes of the party faded into silence. The candles. The cake. The jacket. The applause. The panic attack.

"I should have felt content."

Instead, he wondered what was wrong with him.

All he could think about was the wish he had made.

I just want to know what's missing.

A laugh tried to rise in his throat, but it caught halfway. He had everything—didn't he? A beautiful family. A career people respected. A gorgeous house with a nearly paid-off mortgage.

So why did something still stab at him from the inside—something he couldn't name?

Outside, the wind began to stir, lifting dry leaves and rattling the shutters. Within seconds, it escalated into a full-blown storm. Rain slammed against the windows in heavy, urgent sheets, as if the sky itself had lost control.

A flash of lightning lit up the room—brief, electric, raw.

In that split-second flicker, Brayden felt something wild surge within him. Caged. Restless. Like a truth long buried, clawing at the edges of his chest, begging to be released.

His breath caught. His body tense.

He rolled onto his side, heart pounding beneath the covers.

His chest was tight.
He rolled onto his side and let the darkness pull him under.

Suddenly, he was three again.

Giant, innocent blue eyes.
Soft brown hair. Dimples so deep they made strangers smile.
No awareness of how adorable he looked—just being.

He sat in the sandbox beneath the weeping willow. The air was warm and sweet, full of flowers and fresh earth. Crickets chirped in the garden, birds sang high above, and everything around him felt soft, alive, and humming with connection.

Beside him, giggling in the sand, was Craig—his twin, his mirror, his best friend—wearing the same tiny marine-blue sailor outfit.
Two matching boys. One heartbeat split in two.

Their mother knelt nearby, humming as she pulled weeds.
Toy vehicles lay scattered—some upright, some tipped over, none in a hurry.

Brayden was lost in play.
Every movement slow, clumsy, deliberate.
He felt his body completely—heavy, warm, limbs still figuring things out.
No rush. No goal. No performance.
Only presence.

He glanced at Craig, love radiating from him like heat off a sun-warmed stone.
Not the kind of love that needed to be spoken or earned—
but the kind that simply *was.*

They breathed the same sweet air, thick with stillness and possibility.
Moments passed in joyful silence, their connection louder than words.
Golden dust swirled through sunbeams above them,
particles suspended like angels watching over them.
Shimmering dragonflies drifted through the air—
messengers from some invisible realm.

No need to speak.
No need to think.
Just the soft hum of being alive together.

Joy expanded in the space between them—pure, effortless, unfiltered.
Contentment without a name.
Wholeness without a single thought.
No longing.
No fear.
Just two little boys sitting in perfect peace.

And it wasn't just a memory.
It was truth.
And Brayden felt it—hovering above his younger self like a ghost.
Not as an idea—
but as the part of him that had never left.

But then—something shifted.
Not suddenly.
Not violently.
Just a flicker.
A soft pulling away.

Time sped up.
They were four. Then five. Then six.

The sandbox remained.
The yard still buzzed with aliveness.
But something inside the moment had changed.

Brayden still played. Still laughed.
But the laughter no longer shook his whole chest.
His movements turned quicker. Less grounded.
He began to watch himself—
to wonder how he looked.
To wonder if he was doing it right.

He used to feel the cool sand press into his legs,
the sun stretch across his arms,
the rhythm of his breath sway like a lullaby.

But now...
his breath stayed high in his chest.
His limbs tensed more often.
His tummy felt tight for reasons he couldn't name.

He was learning to leave himself.
Not in one big moment—
but in quiet, invisible steps.

It happened every time he blinked back tears.
Every time he said *"I'm fine"* while something inside him ached.
Every time he heard:

"Don't cry."
"Be strong."
"You're okay."
"Big boys don't act like that."

The words weren't meant to harm.
They came like rules for survival.

But they taught him something else:

Your feelings are too much.
Your truth is inconvenient.
Hide it. Shrink it. Lock it away.

So he did.

The feelings still came—strong as ever—
but now they had nowhere to go.

He began to store them.
Tuck them deep.
Smile through the sting.

Craig kept chasing dragonflies.
Every time, it felt like an invitation—
a reminder to return to something Brayden didn't know he was losing.

Then the dream shifted again.
And the game began.

Memories flickered—
birthday candles, scraped knees, mud-covered shoes, snow forts, school bells—
until everything blurred.

The enthusiasm… fading.
The sparkle… dulling.

Brayden saw it with heartbreaking clarity:
the slow erosion of wonder.

It didn't happen all at once.
It was the drip, drip, drip of voices shaping him.

Be quiet.
You're overreacting.
Get over it.

Not true.
Not free.
Just… manageable.

He learned to read his parents like weather maps—
scanning for storms, predicting moods.

He absorbed their tension, their silence, their disappointment…
without ever understanding why.

But he didn't need to understand.
He just needed to survive.

And survival meant more than food or shelter.
It meant love. Connection. Approval.

So he morphed—
into the boy they could tolerate.
Especially once Mom started drinking.

At school, the pressure deepened.
Blend in.
Don't ask the wrong questions.
Perform. Follow.

And so the little boy who once chased dragonflies barefoot under sunbeams...
started walking slower.
Talking less.
Looking down instead of up.

His shoulders rounded.
His body stiffened.
His heart… closed.

Not because he was weak—
but because staying open in a world of sharp edges and cold silences
felt like dragging bare skin across barbed wire.

And that was the real tragedy:
Not one moment of abuse—
but a thousand tiny cuts from the hands of the unaware.
The kind of careless shaping that comes not from monsters…
…but from the sleepwalking of those too wounded to see.

Then—another shift.

His teenage bedroom. Dim. Cluttered.
A glowing video game console in the corner.

Fifteen-year-old Brayden sat hunched over a controller, eyes blank.
Onscreen, an armored warrior hacked through enemies.
Explosions. Chaos.

But the boy wasn't excited.
He was empty.

I have to get to the next level, he thought, glassy-eyed. *I have to win.*

Adult Brayden hovered close, desperate.
"It's just a game," he whispered. "Don't get lost in the game."

But the boy didn't hear.
His fingers only gripped tighter.

Suddenly, the screen flashed red. *Game over.*

Teenage Brayden screamed, hurled the controller at the wall,
then collapsed onto the bed, sobbing silently.

And then—the glitch.

The room shimmered. A bright flash.

The boy looked up.
But it wasn't Brayden anymore.

It was Craig.
Smiling.

"I'm still here, bro," he said, warm and steady. "Happy birthday."

Brayden gasped—and woke up.

The room was dark. Silent.
His heart thundered. His breath came in short bursts.

What the hell was that?

He sat up, hands to his face, trying to shake it off.
But something told him this wasn't just a dream.
Not this time.

Something had opened.
And something was waiting.

A memory. A shadow.
A secret he had buried so deeply, he'd nearly forgotten it existed.

But now—after all these years—
it was rising.

Not as a thought.
But as a feeling.

And just like his nosy, impossible-to-ignore neighbor Ron—already rumbling past the window on a riding mower with the sun barely up—
it wasn't going away anytime soon.

Riding the Edge

Brayden jolted awake too early—like a man mid-fall in a dream. Disoriented. Breath tight. Head buzzing.

And there it was again—Ron's mower.

That unmistakable engine grind tore through the morning peace like a chainsaw in a monastery.

Brayden flinched.

Just a dream, he told himself.

But his body knew better.

The shadows of the night clung to him, damp and persistent, like the smoke that lingers long after a fire dies down. Craig's voice still echoed through his ribs:

"I'm still here with you, bro. Happy birthday."

The memory rattled him. His discomfort twisted into irritation—redirected straight at Ron.

"What a jerk," he muttered. "How many times have I asked him to start mowing later on weekends? Three? Four? All he cares about is mowing that stupid lawn every 42 hours."

Brayden had privately nicknamed him Mow Ron. It wasn't kind, but it felt deserved. The man had an obsessive relationship with his lawn and zero regard for the rest of the neighborhood's sanity.

Beside him, Holly slept peacefully, somehow immune to both the mower's noise and Brayden's internal ruckus. He envied her.

"I need air," Brayden whispered. "I can't face the family like this. They'll ask questions. I don't have answers."

He scribbled a quick note on the counter.

Went for a ride. Be back soon. Love you.

Then he slid into his new leather jacket—cool against his skin, the scent of fresh hide grounding him in something real—and snuck out the door.

The storm had passed, but its fingerprints were everywhere: broken branches littered the sidewalk, puddles shimmered in the cracks, and the sky looked scrubbed raw. The air was thick with the smell of wet earth and unsettled energy.

But inside him, it hadn't cleared. Not even close.

His Harley sat in the driveway like a coiled dragon, humming with silent loyalty.

While fastening his helmet, Brayden glanced toward Mow Ron, who was now waving cheerfully while flashing an unapologetic smile.

Brayden waved back with all the enthusiasm of a man internally flipping the bird. "Yep," he muttered. "He doesn't give a damn."

He revved the engine—loudly—and peeled off, contributing his own brand of noise pollution.

The Alberta sky stretched wide and blue. Cherry blossoms blurred pink across the fields. Lilac rode the wind. But none of it reached him.

He twisted the throttle. Hard.

That voice in his head—the one he had always assumed was just him—was already warming up.

You're overreacting.
Pull yourself together.
What would Jake think?
Don't be dramatic. You're a grown man.

It was just a dream. Just a dream. Just a dream.

It was like living with a bossy roommate who never paid rent and had somehow gained squatter's rights inside his mind.

Brayden didn't argue. He just rode. Faster. Let the wind scream for him.

But the voice wasn't finished.

Seriously? A panic attack at your own birthday party? What are you, twelve?
You're slipping. Losing it.
Pull it together before someone notices.

He clenched his jaw and gunned the throttle again. The engine roared like it wanted to swallow the voice whole.

Why now? Why Craig?

Don't open that box, the voice warned. *You locked it up for a reason.*

Then why is it breaking open?

The road curved. Brayden leaned hard into it, the wind clawing at his face.

Normally, riding brought peace. Normally, it would sweep the clutter from his mind and leave him quiet.

Not today.

Today, it only stirred the dust.

And lately, there was so much dust. So much he couldn't name.

Something had been brewing in him for years—long before the party, even before the dream. A kind of heavy restlessness that had started quietly but had only intensified in the aftermath of the pandemic. He hadn't spoken much about it—who had? But the weight was real. The fatigue. The restlessness. The sense that the world had tilted slightly off its axis and never quite corrected.

People didn't talk the same anymore. Everyone seemed distracted, distrustful, suspicious of each other's opinions. Conversations felt like minefields. Empathy had thinned. And somewhere in the static of it all, something essential had gone missing.

He couldn't name it. But he felt it in his bones.

It's like we all came back, he thought, but something didn't.

He'd tried to shake it off. Get back to normal. Power through. Be grateful. But the pressure had kept building—quietly, invisibly—until his body staged a full-blown mutiny at his own birthday party.

He hadn't told anyone. Not even Holly. Just collapsed in the bathroom with the walls closing in, heart racing, eyes wide. A trapped animal in a gilded cage.

And now, riding alone, trying to outrun it—it was still there.

The same tightness gripped his chest. His breath shortened. His fingers trembled against the handlebars.

Get it together, he told himself. You're fine. Just tired. Just stressed.

No, whispered something deeper. *You're not fine. You've just been pretending to be for too long.*

And then it hit him—he was having an argument with himself. Listening and responding to his own mind.

The insight landed like a crack through the center of his fragile psyche.

He didn't know what scared him more—that the voice might be wrong… or that it might fully be in control.

He had never once questioned it.

The running monologue. The inner commentator who had been narrating his life since childhood.

It had always been there, and he had always obeyed it like gospel.

But what if it wasn't telling the truth?

What if it never had?

He never challenged its narrative.

Never asked whether it had any credentials.

He had spent his entire life taking orders from a mental intercom system that sounded authoritative but might just be an overcaffeinated gremlin in a headset.

He tightened his grip until his knuckles went white, as if squeezing harder could shut it up.

You don't get to evict voices like that. They don't pack their bags and go. They linger. Set up camp. Decorate. Start charging rent.

The road curved again.

And just for a moment, Brayden caught something in his side mirror.

A flicker. A shape. Someone riding behind him.

He tensed and glanced over his shoulder.

No one there.

He looked again. Nothing but trees and road.

But a few minutes later—it happened again.

Something in the corner of his eye. A figure trailing him. But when he turned—empty road. Nothing at all.

His heart knocked hard against his ribs.

Was he being followed?

Or was something following him from the inside out?

Jake's house finally appeared in the distance, silhouetted against the gold-edged morning.

Brayden pulled into the gravel driveway and cut the engine.

The silence that followed slammed into him like a wall.

He just sat there. Hands frozen. Heart racing. Mind… loud.

Then slowly, boots crunching on gravel, he stepped toward the front door.

He knocked. Twice.

A hollow echo.

And for the first time in his life, Brayden wasn't afraid of what someone else might say.

He was terrified of what *the voice* might say next.

Would it keep pretending everything was fine—even with his best friend?
Why did vulnerability feel like a liability, like something that could unravel his whole existence?
When did he stop being real and become this polished, fearful version of himself?
Had the tyrannical voice been leading him there all along?
And why?

Brayden felt so lost, he could barely breathe.
Then—slowly—the door began to open.

Chaos Theory

Back at the house, David was the first one up—but not because he'd slept well. He hadn't really slept at all.

His eyes felt like sandpaper. His thumbs? Cramping. His brain? A burnt-out jellyfish.

He'd broken the *no phones in bedrooms* rule again—third time this week, but who was counting? Hopefully he could sneak through undetected. If not, he was ready with a fallback plan: the sleepwalking defense.

"No idea how it got there, Mom and Dad. Did you know teens are more prone to sleepwalking than adults?"

He'd rehearsed it in his head, even practiced looking dazed. But right now, his priority was caffeine. Strong caffeine. The adult kind his parents totally disapproved of.

He crept into the kitchen, opened the sacred bean cupboard, and pulled out the forbidden bag. The espresso machine sputtered to life, hissing like it disapproved too.

A note sat on the counter in Brayden's quick, messy scrawl:

Went for a ride. Be back soon. Love you.

David raised an eyebrow. Huh. His dad only took early rides when something was bothering him. Oh well—more coffee for him.

He sipped his steaming mug like it was survival juice, then collapsed onto the couch and started scrolling—reels, *Italian brain-rot,* roasts, endless clips of people pretending they had it all together.

He didn't think too hard about why he was always online. It wasn't like he *needed* validation from strangers. Not exactly. He just liked comments. And reactions. And that fleeting feeling that maybe, somewhere, someone saw him.

What David couldn't yet see was the sadness underneath it all. The ache. The quiet loneliness lodged somewhere deep in his bones.
He was a master of using humor to sidestep uncomfortable feelings—but

underneath the jokes, he just wanted to belong.
Really belong.

His childhood had been full of little stings—rejection, mockery, being the odd one out. Eventually, he started believing it was his fault. Maybe he *was* weird. Maybe people were right to leave him out.

He didn't know yet that these buried beliefs were driving so much of his behavior—that without them, his self-esteem wouldn't feel so paper-thin.

For now, he just scrolled, hoping the glow of the screen might soothe the parts of him that felt disconnected.

Upstairs, Lily hovered between two worlds.

She wasn't fully asleep anymore—but not awake, either. Drifting in a twilight space where time felt thick and her body didn't quite belong to her. The room was quiet, still wrapped in that early morning hush. Yet something shifted.

A presence stood at her bedside.

She didn't open her eyes all the way—just enough to make out a tall, masculine shape in the soft gold haze of morning light. He looked like Dad. Same height. Same outline. Same gentle weight in the room.

"Dad…" she murmured. "It's Saturday… you don't need to wake me up."

The figure didn't move. Just stood there.

Lily rolled over and pulled the blanket to her chin. A chill swept down her back, but she dismissed it.

When she finally sat up for real, the room was empty.
She didn't think much of it. He'd probably just gone downstairs.

But something else had already crept into her chest—tight and cold and familiar.

What if they posted more?

That sharp, fluttery dread stirred in her stomach. The kind that showed up *before* she even checked her phone.

The fear of opening Instagram.
The fear of a new tag.
The fear of another "harmless" post she wasn't meant to see—but saw anyway.

Another inside joke she wasn't part of.
Another filtered photo that made her feel like garbage in comparison.

Like her big brother David, Lily just wanted to feel loved. Accepted. And for as long as she could remember, it felt like that only happened online—through the posts, the pictures, the likes. That was where you mattered. That was where you existed.

Or so she'd believed.

She hadn't expected people to be so cruel.
She hadn't expected the algorithms to cheer them on.
It never crossed her mind that a *machine* could profit off her pain, off her need to be seen.

She slid off the bed and shuffled to the mirror, heart heavy.
Checked her forehead. Her chin. Her cheeks.
No new pimples.

Thank God.

Still, her reflection gave her nothing back.
No approval. No comfort. No reason to feel okay.

She frowned, pulled her sleeves over her hands, and padded downstairs.
Already, she was carrying the weight of someone twice her age—
and somehow, this was just… normal.

In the kitchen, David was still slouched on the couch, watching a video of an Italian guy screaming in operatic rage about someone stealing his pet goat.

Lily grabbed her phone from the shelf and poured a bowl of cereal, extra milk to drown out her thoughts.

"I would've slept in longer," she said, "if Dad hadn't come in and creepily woke me up."

David didn't look away from the screen. "Dad? He's been gone since before I woke up. Left a note on the counter."

Lily paused, spoon in hand. "Wait—what? He's not home?"

"Nope. Said he went for a ride."

Lily's eyes narrowed for a second. "Huh… weird. I must've still been dreaming then."

She shrugged it off and sat down at the table, chewing slowly. But the chill from earlier hadn't fully left. Neither had the dread curled up inside her, waiting for her to check her phone.

Before Lily could turn on her phone, the calm shattered.

Maggie thundered down the stairs like a Broadway diva in crisis.

"Oh my god, where *is* everyone? I swear, if either of you mess this up for me—"

She stormed into the kitchen, hair curled to commercial-level perfection, wearing a red tank top that read *Boss.*

"Just a heads-up," she announced, tossing her giant tote bag onto the island. "Ava, Madison, and Zoe are coming over in like five minutes to run through our choreography for grad night. So if you could both act *normal* for once, that would be awesome."

David didn't even look up. "Define normal."

Maggie scowled. "Not being weird. Not doing that thing where you embarrass me on purpose."

"Oh, you mean *being ourselves*?" he said, setting down his coffee mug with dramatic flair. "That's a tall order."

And before Maggie could launch her next tirade, David grabbed the bunch of bananas from the counter, plopped it on his head like a crown, and started walking in exaggerated slow motion around the kitchen island.

Lily cracked up, unable to resist. She grabbed the whipped cream canister from the fridge, squirted a foamy dollop onto her nose, crossed her eyes, and struck a superhero pose.

"Behold," she announced in a nasal voice, "Banana King and Whipped Goddess—protectors of weirdness, banishers of conformity."

"Oh my *god*," Maggie gasped, nearly dropping her phone. "You guys are such CHILDREN. Can you *please* not ruin this? You're making a mess! My friends will be here any second!"

"You say that like it's a threat," David mumbled, still balancing the banana crown like royalty.

At that moment, Holly walked in, designer purse in one hand, car keys in the other.

She stopped in her tracks.

"Lily, are you planning on going to badminton with whipped cream on your nose?"

Lily yelped, grabbed a napkin, and wiped her face.

"Oh shoot—I forgot about badminton! Do I *have* to go?"

"Yes," Holly said without missing a beat. "Do you know how much we pay for those classes? We're leaving in ten minutes."

The doorbell rang.

Maggie screamed internally (and maybe a little externally) as she sprinted to the front door.

She flung it open with theatrical enthusiasm.

And in came Ava, Madison, and Zoe, all hair flips, crop tops and acrylic nails, looking like they had just stepped out of a salon.

"Heyyy!" Zoe squealed. "Oh my gosh, I love your kitchen! It's so like… minimalistic but expensive."

They dropped their bags and immediately broke into choreography, bursting into the chorus of:

"It's gonna be a good, good night!"

David leaned against the fridge, arms crossed, deadpan.

Ava spotted him and smirked.

"Hey David, wanna make us some coffees? We'll let you take a selfie with us."

He blinked slowly, as if processing a foreign language.

"Really?" he said. "Wow. What a privilege. I'm *eternally* grateful. However, I have slightly more important business to attend to… like plucking my nose hairs."

He bowed and walked off with Shakespearean grace.

Holly clapped once. "Alright, Lily—grab your stuff. Let's go. We're going to be late."

Lily gulped down the last of her cereal, phone still untouched beside her bowl.

"Coming," she mumbled.

And just like that, the house split in two—half chaos, half choreography, with the weight of unseen storms still hanging in the air.
No one said it out loud.
But everyone was fighting something.

Everyone was just trying to outrun the ache in whatever way made sense to them—scrolling, snapping, controlling, caffeinating.
Some with silence. Some with noise.
All of them searching for relief they couldn't name.

Funny how nothing ever seemed to soothe it for very long.

Jake's Lair

The door creaked open, and there stood Jake in pajama pants, an oversized hoodie, and hair that looked like it had hosted a small lightning storm.

"Well, if it isn't the birthday boy," he said, grinning as he took in Brayden's black leather jacket. "Midlife crisis looks good on you."

Brayden gave a tired half-smile. "Had to get out for a bit."

Jake stepped aside and waved him in. "Come on in. You look like you've just seen a ghost—or ten. Coffee's on. Sarah's still out cold."

Trix, Jake's golden retriever, padded over with his tail wagging gently, ears perked. He nudged Brayden's leg with his nose, then—sensing something—started licking his hand. Then his wrist. Then, suddenly, his face.

"Whoa—okay, Trix. I get it," Brayden said, laughing through the overwhelm.

But the dog wasn't joking. He licked Brayden's cheek again and again, like he was trying to pull him out of his own head.

"Alright, Trix," Jake said, snapping his fingers gently. "That's enough. Sit."

Trix obeyed, settling beside the couch with a soft huff, eyes still on Brayden like he was monitoring a storm.

The house smelled like eggs, burnt toast, and that earthy, lived-in scent of second-hand furniture and dog hair. The kitchen light buzzed softly, and the glow of a paused Netflix screen spilled into the hallway. Everything about Jake's place was a little messy, a little warm, and exactly the kind of grounding imperfection Brayden hadn't realized he needed.

Jake handed him a steaming mug. "Drink this. You look like you've been up all night solving the mystery of existence."

Brayden took a sip. "Didn't sleep much," he muttered. "Weird dream."

Jake flopped onto the couch and patted the spot beside him. "Perfect timing. I'm watching this documentary that's basically a spiritual sledgehammer. Come get your brain broken."

Feels like it already is, Brayden thought.

He sank into the couch, the cushions groaning beneath him like they, too, were reluctant to be awake. His body felt like wet cement. Heavy. Unresponsive. In the dream, he'd felt so free—weightless, alive. Now, even lifting his mug required effort.

Jake gestured to the TV. "So this guy—Dr. Eben Alexander. Neurosurgeon. Harvard. Hardcore science guy. Didn't believe in anything woo-woo until it happened to him."

Brayden raised an eyebrow. "Let me guess. Tunnel of light. Choir of angels. Cotton candy clouds."

Jake smirked. "Pretty much, yeah. Except he didn't believe any of it. Until he flatlined."

Brayden took another sip of coffee. The bitterness grounded him, but his brain was already bracing for impact—defensive, skeptical, slightly annoyed.

Here we go. Cue dramatic music, a ghostly montage, and a best-selling book deal.

The thoughts came fast, uninvited—like pop-up ads from the rational side of his brain. Not chosen. Just… programmed. They sounded like common sense. Like logic. Like the cool, detached voice of his inner engineer, always ready to dismantle nonsense before it made it past security.

He had never questioned the voice.

It had always been there—narrating, analyzing, mocking, calculating.

But lately—especially this morning—it felt less like *truth* and more like… a *script.*

Why does this voice never shut up?
Why can't I turn it off?

He was trapped in a one-man conversation he'd never actually agreed to—but had somehow been part of for years.

Who's doing the talking?

The screen flickered, drawing him back.

Dr. Eben Alexander appeared—clean-cut, articulate, radiating that weird mix of scientific credibility and spiritual calm.

"I didn't believe in any of this," he said. "Not until it happened to me."

He talked about falling into a coma from a brain infection—bacterial meningitis. His entire neocortex had shut down—basically, the thinking part of the brain was offline. No awareness, no memories, no dreaming. Nothing should've been happening at all.

And yet… what he described sounded more vivid than anything Brayden had ever felt awake.

Colors that didn't exist in this world. Sounds that went through him, not around him. And a feeling of being completely, utterly held—like he was wrapped in some giant current of love.

"Consciousness is not confined to the brain," Dr. Alexander said. "It transcends the boundaries of our physical existence."

Brayden stiffened.

Jake nudged him. "Here's the kicker. When he woke up, his neocortex was still inactive. Zero brain activity. But he remembered *everything.*"

Brayden frowned. "And you believe this?"

Jake shrugged. "I'm a nurse. I've seen enough weird stuff to stop pretending the physical world is all there is. People in comas knowing things, describing stuff they shouldn't be able to… It happens."

Brayden stayed quiet. He watched. He listened.

"There is no true separation between the physical and spiritual realms," the doctor continued.

The line landed like a punch to the chest.

His logical brain rushed to armor up.

Misfiring neurons.
Hallucination.
Wishful thinking.

But somewhere deeper—quiet and ignored for years—something stirred.

He didn't believe it.

Not yet.

But he couldn't just laugh it off this time.

Jake reached for the remote and muted the TV. The silence filled the room like fog.

He glanced at Brayden, then looked away.
Then back again.

"I've never told you this," Jake said, his voice softer now. "But something happened to me too. A long time ago."

Brayden turned toward him, more alert than he'd been in days.

Trix sensed the shift and let out a soft whimper of anticipation.

Jake didn't speak again—not yet.

But the look in his eyes said everything:
Get ready.

Chapter 2

The Glitch in the Code

System Disruption

It had been a solid hour and a half since Holly and Lily left for badminton—and now they were back, shoes squeaking on the tiled entrance as they stepped into what could only be described as a high-gloss, teen-infused tornado.

The house had been officially *taken over.*

Hair clips, scrunchies, lip gloss tubes, phones, jackets, open water bottles, half-eaten protein bars, and what looked like a full contour kit littered the floor, the couches, the banister, and every surface of the main floor.

"3, 2, 1—GO!" Maggie shouted from the living room.

Music exploded from the speaker.

"It's gonna be a good night… a good, good night!"

The girls launched into their routine, all energy and precision and high ponytails.

Holly and Lily froze at the entrance, unable to move past the whirl of limbs and choreography now taking over the hallway.

They stood awkwardly, watching.

Lily's eyes tracked the older girls in silence. They looked flawless. Confident. Synchronized. Their clothes clung just right, their makeup looked perfect, and their laughter had that breezy sparkle Lily couldn't fake if she tried.

She told herself it didn't matter.
That she didn't care.

But somewhere inside, a quiet ache bloomed.

I wish I looked like that.
I wish I belonged somewhere like that.

It wasn't a loud thought. More like a secret whisper tucked behind her ribs. The kind of voice that spoke without words—just a tightening in the chest, a twist in the stomach, a sudden weight she didn't ask to carry.

She didn't notice the thought.
But she *felt* it.

The song ended with a dramatic spin and jump, landing on the final beat.

Boom.

Applause echoed—only from the entrance.

"Thanks, Mrs. Montgomery," Madison called, slightly breathless. "It's coming along!"

"You girls look amazing," Holly said, clapping. "Is your dad not back yet?"

"Nope," Maggie replied. "Still just us." She clapped her hands together. "Alright ladies, one more time, then let's call it a day!"

The music started again. The girls reassembled.

And then, David appeared.

He strolled down the stairs like he was entering a stage, holding his phone mounted on a mini tripod pointed straight at his face. His voice switched into his full *influencer mode.*

"Alright guys, get ready for this—what you're about to witness is a once-in-a-lifetime performance. Totally free. Donations accepted. Welcome to high definition chaos!"

He flipped the camera toward the dancers mid-routine.

All four girls screamed.

"DAVID—NO!"

"DON'T FILM US!"

"STOP!"

They shrieked, ducked, and dashed into the dining room, covering their faces like he was the paparazzi and they were trying to protect their identities.

David howled with laughter. "And *that*, folks, is how you clear the space and reclaim your house from your sister and her minions!"

The girls heard him. And that was it.

They charged back in with throw pillows.

David tried to retreat, phone still rolling, but the pillows came at him from every direction. One caught him square in the neck. Another nearly took out his camera.

"Violence! I'm being assaulted on live!" he laughed, still filming.

"CUT IT OUT!" Holly shouted from the front hallway. "ENOUGH!"

She walked over and looked straight into David's phone. "If there are any adults watching this, help! I'm trapped in a house with six teenagers!"

Right on cue, Lily entered from the kitchen with whipped cream on her nose again—like it was totally normal.

David doubled over. "Oh man. This content is gold."

Maggie was livid. "I *swear*, if you post that, I will sue you."

"Relax," David said. "It's just a live. Still rolling. Smile, Maggie! This is your big break. Don't blow it."

Maggie lunged forward, grabbed his phone, slapped her hand over the lens, and hit the red button.

"HEY! Careful with that, Magpie!" David shouted.

"ENOUGH," Holly snapped. "David—go do your chores. Leave the girls alone. Maggie—pick up the pillows, and you girls can cool down in the living room. Lily—grab your dirty laundry. We're doing a load right now."

The doorbell rang.

Holly threw her hands in the air. "Now what?"

She opened the door.

"Oh!" Her face lit up. "My massage oils! I've been waiting all week for these."

She took the package reverently, like it was sacred, and carried it to the counter with the care of someone handling precious cargo.

"I can't *wait* to smell each one," she said, already slicing open the box with a butter knife. "My clients are going to love these…"

She unwrapped the little glass bottles like they were buried treasure. Sandalwood. Neroli. Citrus. Lavender. Her whole body seemed to relax.

The mood shift was instant.

All the yelling, the mess, the adolescent chaos—forgotten.

This was her sanctuary. Pretty smells. New purchases. Her small but reliable dose of joy.

Retail therapy.

It wasn't a conscious thing. Just… something she did. Something she needed. A little pleasure to smooth over the noise.

And today, it had arrived just in time.

Beyond the Glitch

Jake had just muted the TV and was holding the remote like a statue, eyes distant, lost in thought.

"I've never told you this before, Brayden" he said, voice low. "But something happened to me too. A long time ago."

Brayden glanced sideways, his fingers tightening around the coffee mug.

Trix lifted his head from the rug, ears twitching. He rose slowly, padded over to Brayden's feet, and leaned gently against his leg.

Jake looked hesitant, like he wasn't sure if he should continue. Then he exhaled and dove in.

"I was eight. My grandmother had just died, but no one had told me yet. That night, I woke up at exactly 2:22 a.m. Just… opened my eyes. And she was there."

Brayden blinked. "There?"

Jake nodded. "Standing at the foot of my bed. She wasn't glowing or anything. She looked like herself—just softer. Almost like… a hologram. But real. More real than real. I wasn't scared at all. I felt calm."

Brayden tried to focus on Jake's voice, but his mind had other plans.

A sharp flash.

Craig's face—sudden, strobing, distorted.

Laughing. Then gone.

Then back again.

Eyes too bright. Mouth open mid-sentence. No sound.

Brayden flinched. His jaw locked.

What the hell was that?

Jake went on, unaware. "She smiled at me. Told me not to be afraid. Said she'd always be with me."

Another flash—Craig in the grass, dragonflies spinning around him.

Then—Craig older. Paler. Still.

Craig vanishing in a blink of static.

Brayden's chest tightened. His shirt clung to his back. Sweat pooled at the base of his neck.

Trix stood up fully and licked Brayden's hand once. Then again. When Brayden didn't respond, the dog pressed a paw onto his knee and gave a quiet whine.

Jake glanced over. "You okay?"

Brayden nodded too quickly. "Yeah. Yeah, I'm fine."

Trix didn't seem convinced. He licked Brayden's face gently, insistently, like he was trying to calm down a skittish animal. Brayden's eyes stayed locked on the screen, unmoving.

Jake didn't push. Just went on, softer now. "The next morning, I looked at my clock—it had stopped at 2:22. Just… frozen. And later, I found out that was the exact time she passed."

Brayden could feel it now—pressure mounting inside him like a sealed valve rattling from the inside. His breath came shorter. Shallower. His palms were damp.

On the TV, the next interview rolled. Captions scrolled silently across the bottom of the screen.

"I felt more alive than I ever had before. There was no fear. Just this overwhelming sense of love…"

Brayden stared at the words, but they felt foreign. Distant. Like someone else's dream in someone else's language.

Another image.

Craig. Sitting beside him at the edge of the creek.

Then gone.

Then a flicker—Craig behind the wheel of a car that wasn't moving.

Stop. Please stop.

"I didn't want to come back," read the next line on the television. "But I was told it wasn't my time."

Brayden swallowed hard. His legs were tense. Every muscle in his body braced like a soldier in a minefield.

Jake leaned back, arms crossed, watching the screen peacefully. "They all say the same thing, man. The light. The love. Like they were more awake there than they ever were here."

Brayden didn't respond. He couldn't.

The voice in his head wasn't just commenting now—it was unraveling.

You need to move. Get up. Get out. Before it happens again.

Jake turned to him, brow furrowing. "Seriously, are you okay?"

Brayden stood too fast. The mug rattled against the table as he set it down.

Trix moved in front of him, tail low, blocking the path between Brayden and the door.

Brayden stepped to the side. Trix stepped with him.

"Hey, buddy," Jake said gently. "It's okay. Sit."

Trix hesitated, gave Brayden one last lick on the hand, and reluctantly obeyed, settling down with a worried groan.

"I gotta go," Brayden said, almost breathless. "I—I just need some air."

Jake blinked. "Okay. Sure. You good to ride?"

Brayden nodded, already halfway to the door. "Yeah. Just… I'll call you later."

He stepped out into the open air. The sunlight hit him like a slap. His lungs pulled in the coolness like he'd just come up from underwater.

Inside, Jake watched the door swing shut.

Something was definitely off.

But knowing Brayden, he figured it was just his engineer brain short-circuiting—trying to solve something that wasn't built for formulas or logic.

What he didn't realize was this:

The cracks in his best friend's psyche were deeper than they looked.

And maybe—just maybe—he shouldn't have let him get back on that bike.

Riding Through the Storm

Brayden didn't remember starting the bike.

One moment, he was at Jake's—lungs clamped shut, heart thudding like it was trying to punch its way out of his chest. The next, he was flying down the backroads, the engine roaring beneath him like something primal and unhinged.

Maybe something was chasing him.

The wind tore at his jacket. The scenery blurred into streaks of gold and green. He leaned hard into each curve, the cool air biting across his cheeks. The bike howled, but it wasn't loud enough to drown out his thoughts.

They were back.

Louder. Faster. Relentless.

What if everything I've ever believed is a lie? What if it's all just a game?

His grip tightened on the handlebars. A wave of nausea rose like oil in his stomach—thick, sour, inescapable. He swallowed hard, but it didn't leave. It pressed up and out, clawing for escape.

And then the flashes came again.

Craig. Laughing.

Craig. Gone.

Craig, flickering like a scrambled signal on a broken TV.

"I'm still here with you, Bro! Happy birthday!"

Not now. Shut up. Not while I'm riding.

He twisted the throttle until the bike screamed beneath him, just to compete with the one screaming inside.

You're not okay. This is happening again. You're unraveling.

His breath quickened. His mind twisted. His body was on fire, tangled in panic and memory.

More flashes.

Craig chasing dragonflies.

Craig eating KFC out of a bucket, grinning like a goof.

Craig yelling at the TV during Halo.

Brayden pushed harder, riding like he could outpace it all—the grief, the memory, the guilt that stalked him like a shadow.

Then—

A voice. Clear. Commanding.

"Pull over, Brayden! STOP!"

He gasped and yanked the handlebars to the right. Tires screamed against the asphalt, skidding to a halt just inches from the shoulder.

Then—out of nowhere—two deer shot across the road.

Graceful. Silent. Untouched.

Brayden sat frozen, the engine idling, his heart jackhammering.

He stumbled off the bike like a man escaping a burning building. His knees gave out as he collapsed onto the roadside, fingers clawing into the earth like it might anchor him to reality.

And then the dam broke.

Craig's face crashed into him—sharp, vivid, unfiltered.

The chess games. The campfires. The nickname—"Brainiac." The laugh that could pull you into it whether you wanted to or not.

And then the other memory.

The one Brayden kept locked behind every smile and every silence.

The ball. The dog. The car. The scream.

"I should've been the one to die!" he shouted, his voice tearing through the quiet like a flare.

"I threw the ball, Craig! You chased it. You chased it—not me!"

His body convulsed with sobs—thirty-six years of unspoken guilt erupting in waves. He pounded the ground, fists slamming into dirt. Again. Again. Rage boiling over.

"WHERE WERE YOU?! I begged for a sign! For *something*! Thirty-six years of silence, and now you show up?!"

The world didn't answer.

The road remained still.

Only the wind responded, rustling the grass like an ancient lullaby.

His energy gave out. He fell back into the earth, arms spread wide, chest heaving like he'd been cracked open.

Above him, the sky yawned—endless and indifferent.

Minutes passed. Maybe more. The pain didn't disappear… but something had shifted.

The pressure was gone.

The storm had emptied.

What was left behind felt hollow. Fragile. But lighter.

His fists unclenched. His breath slowed. Something like peace—not loud or bright, but soft and strange—moved through him like a breeze.

And then… he saw it.

A cloud, delicate and strange, floating just above the treetops.

Long body. Four soft wings.

A dragonfly.

Brayden stared, breath caught in his throat. The shape hovered in the sky, weightless and precise, as if drawn just for him.

He didn't know what it meant.

Not yet.

But something inside him stirred. Like an old rusted gear shifting back into place.

He watched until the cloud dissolved into the blue.

Then, slowly, he climbed back onto his bike. The engine rumbled to life, steadier now—more heartbeat than explosion.

As he pulled back onto the road, one thought followed like a whisper on the wind:

Something strange is happening.

Something I can't name. Something I can't stop.

And if he'd known—if he'd had even the faintest clue how fast everything was about to change—

He might've stayed in that field just a little longer.

Processing

It was like a valve had finally been released—decades of pressure hissing out in one messy, beautiful breakdown. Brayden glanced once more at the vast field behind him, where his rage, his grief, and his guilt now lay scattered like forgotten luggage at a roadside rest stop.

For the first time in decades, he didn't feel like he was carrying it all. His chest felt lighter. His shoulders looser. Even his breath—deeper, easier.

The ride home unfolded in soft colors and stillness. He didn't grip the handlebars like he was bracing for impact. He just rode.

His mind, once a relentless swarm of thoughts, had gone quiet. Not empty—clear. Spacious. Like someone had finally shut off a radio he didn't realize had been blaring in the background for years.

And into that quiet… life flooded in.

The sun warmed his face. The scent of open fields filled his lungs—grassy, earthy, tinged with lilac and dust. The sky stretched wide above him, a deep, undisturbed blue. Even the Harley beneath him pulsed with rhythm—less machine now, more heartbeat. On his lips, the faint taste of salt lingered. His tears. His body had finally let go—muscles unlocked, breath moving like the tide.

He wasn't rushing home. He wasn't running away.

He was just… here.

Riding. Breathing. Alive.

When he pulled into the driveway, Mow Ron was out front waxing (a.k.a. flaunting) his new Maserati convertible.

"That's the bait," Brayden thought. "Somewhere, a half-his-age girlfriend is manifesting as we speak."

The sun had warmed the house to a glow. The windows gleamed. It looked… staged. Like a still from a movie he wasn't sure he belonged in anymore.

Inside, there was warmth. The sweet scent of cinnamon buns. And an eruption of teenage girl energy. The living room was a battlefield of pillows, fuzzy blankets, tangled limbs, and snack debris. Maggie and her friends were sprawled across the sectional in what could only be described as a sacred scrolling ceremony.

Brayden had no idea how much teen mayhem had unfolded under his roof just a short while ago, while he was unraveling in a field of his own. He had narrowly missed the full teen musical production: choreography, screaming, livestreaming, whipped cream, and at least one dramatic exit.

"Hey, Dad!" Maggie called, ponytail bouncing. "Did you see Ron's new toy?"

"I sure did. Hard to miss," Brayden said, stepping out of his boots and into the hormonal tornado.

Ava looked up. "Wait—is that the jacket?"

Madison leaned forward. "Okay, okay. That's actually fire."

Brayden did a slow spin, striking a mock-model pose. "Birthday gift. I've officially entered my leather jacket era."

Zoe, eyes still on her phone, added dryly, "You look like a retired action star who runs a conspiracy podcast."

He chuckled, leaning against the doorway, absorbing the scene like a tourist in a parallel universe.

His mind remained quiet. His senses, alive. The shimmer of sun across a glass. The rustle of socks on carpet. The perfume and lotion and half-whispered secrets. Someone's AirPods leaking out a song he couldn't name but recognized from every mall food court in existence.

They're like characters in a video game called TeenWorld, he thought. All running the same script.

"Did you see her Insta story? Oh my God, I can't even."

"She's so fake. I literally can't."

Scroll. Swipe. Gasp. Repeat.

But Brayden wasn't judging. In fact, there was something oddly tender about it. The predictability. The performance. The safety. They were synced like murmuring birds—choreographed chaos with no need for a leader.

Maggie caught his gaze. "You good?"

"Yeah," he said, smiling. "Just taking it all in."

She squinted at him suspiciously, then shrugged and returned to scrolling.

She has no idea what just happened out there, he thought.

Thank God.

Then—Maggie's phone lit up.

She gasped. "OH MY GOD."

"What?!" Ava's voice went full emergency.

Maggie held up the phone like a sacred relic. "It's him. Samuel just texted me."

Screams.

All four girls shrieked in unison, a perfect sonic boom. Precious the cat, horrified, launched from the windowsill and vanished down the hallway with her tail puffed like a duster.

"You scared her!" Ava yelled.

"She'll recover," said Madison through laughter-tears.

Maggie stared at her screen like it was showing her a vision of the future—her entire romantic destiny unfolding in pixels.

Suddenly, David walked around the corner wearing latex gloves, safety glasses, an apron, and holding a sponge—his designer outfit for cleaning the bathroom. Under his breath, he sang, "Maggie and Samuel, sittin' in a tree… K-I-S-S-I-N-G…"

The spell shattered. Maggie's dreamy gaze snapped into a death glare. "Shut up, David. Go back to scrubbing!"

She hurled a throw pillow at him again without warning. It missed by a mile and knocked over a water bottle instead.

David burst out laughing. "You've gotta work on that aim if you want to impress Samuel."

Brayden stood at the edge of the room, watching.

He didn't say a word.

No raised voice. No lecture. No classic Dad sigh.

He was just there—still, steady, present.

And somehow, that was enough.

His posture alone seemed to shift the energy in the room. Maggie and David noticed. Not with guilt, exactly—but with the kind of quiet awareness that settles in when you realize someone's actually paying attention.

Without saying a thing, Brayden's body language calmly commanded them: *Take it easy. Be kind.*

The tension fizzled.

David adjusted his gloves. Maggie tucked her phone under a blanket.

Brayden exhaled softly, almost without realizing it.

He had emptied out the storm.

But now, the real question hovered in the quiet:

What was about to fill its place?

Engineering the Game

Brayden left the girls to their dopamine doses and wandered into the kitchen.

He moved on instinct—pouring the milk, grinding the beans, warming the steamer. His hands knew what to do, like they were executing preloaded instructions. No hesitation. No thought.

The grinder whirred. The scent of fresh beans sweetened the air—earthy, rich, comforting. The steamer hissed softly, building pressure like a breath held too long.

He poured the espresso, then the milk—watching as the dark and light spiraled together in slow, silken motion. It reminded him of acrylic paints blending on wet paper. Two distinct parts softening into something new.

He took a breath. Deep. Even.

Another program, he thought. *Perfectly timed muscle memory. Like riding the Harley. Like tying a shoe. Like bracing for disappointment.*

How many moments like this have I lived without actually living them?

He lifted the mug to his lips, then paused, steam curling up into his face. His mind, still quiet but gently reactivating, began to map.

Inputs. Outputs. Triggers. Reactions. Scripts.

The patterns were everywhere. In the way people spoke. In their laughs, their apologies, their sighs. In Maggie and her friends, echoing each other without missing a beat.

They're like characters in a simulation, he thought. *Running synchronized code. Performing social rituals like sacred loops.*

He could still hear them:

"Did you see her Insta story? Oh my God, I can't even."
"I know, right? She's like… so fake."
"Literally. I can't even handle it."

Even their micro-expressions were in sync. Matching inflections. Flawless rhythm. Like avatars following a precise social algorithm.

And then the dream flashed again—his teenage self, clutching a controller, immersed in the game, convinced it was all real.

What if what I've believed to be life… is just a program?
A hyper-real simulation so immersive, I forgot it was a simulation?

He didn't really know what that meant. But the thought latched on. Something about it felt more like remembering than discovering.

In his quiet distraction, his elbow bumped the mug. The coffee sloshed. Teetered. And then—gravity took over.

The mug tilted. Warm liquid spilled across the counter and splashed onto the floor in a slow, cinematic arc.

Brayden tensed.

And there it was.

That voice. Sharp. Immediate.

You idiot. Watch what you're doing!

So familiar. So automatic.

Then—unexpectedly—a second voice.

Chill, man. No use crying over spilt milk.

He froze, towel in hand.

Wait… which voice is real?

One was angry. One was casual.
Neither felt like truth.

Do I even need to listen to either of them?

Before he could answer, Precious leapt onto the counter like a striped missile, her tongue already sampling the warm puddle.

"Down, Precious! No!" Brayden snapped, his irritation flaring on autopilot.

She jumped down without remorse, tail flicking in defiance.

He sighed, then resumed wiping the counter in silence, brow furrowed.

As he tossed the damp towel onto the counter, his eyes landed on a magnet-pinned photo stuck to the fridge. It was a picture of him and Holly from years ago—arms around each other, both smiling wide, younger, brighter.

He stared at it for a long moment.

How many of our behaviors are just programming too?

Assumptions. Expectations. The roles we fall into, the masks we forget we're wearing. The automatic reactions in an argument. The silences we fill with old scripts.

Had they ever truly seen each other… or just memorized the parts?

The thought gave him pause, like stepping onto a staircase and realizing one of the steps wasn't where it was supposed to be.

Re-enter: Precious.

The Bengal cat slinked into the kitchen with calculated elegance, her movements smooth as liquid silk. Nose twitching at the scent of milk, she paused like royalty surveying her kingdom. Then, with regal confidence, she dipped her tongue into the small puddle on the floor—claiming it as her own.

Brayden raised an eyebrow. "The last thing we need is a caffeinated cat. You're already vibrating at the speed of sound."

Precious ignored him entirely, tail flicking with royal disregard.

He leaned against the counter, sipping the last lukewarm inch of his coffee. His eyes drifted to the window, unfocused. The light had shifted—softened. For a moment, everything was still.

Then—

"Hi Daddy!" Lily's voice rang out as she emerged from the basement, arms wrapped around a laundry basket that nearly swallowed her whole.

She dropped it to the floor and ran toward him, throwing her arms around his waist.

Brayden smiled, wrapping her in a hug. "Hi, sweetheart! Did you go to badminton this morning?"

"I did," she said brightly, "and the weirdest thing happened. About halfway through, you suddenly popped into my mind—for, like… no reason. And then I started feeling really weird."

He pulled back slightly, brows drawing together. "Weird how?"

"My heart started racing. I couldn't breathe. I felt dizzy and had to sit down. I felt really sad, and I had no idea why. Then… a few minutes later, it all just stopped. I felt totally fine. Totally relieved."

Before he could respond, Holly stepped into the kitchen, phone in one hand and a smoothie in the other.

"Hi Brayden! Everything okay this morning?" She glanced at him with casual concern. "You know how intuitive Lily's always been."

Brayden straightened instinctively.
Guard up.
Smile on.

"Yeah, everything was fine," he said quickly. "I just went to visit Jake. Lily, did you have enough to eat before badminton?"

She tilted her head, sensing the shift. "Yeah, Dad. But… I really felt like you weren't okay."

He placed a hand gently on her shoulder. "Don't worry, sweetie. You can see there's nothing to worry about."

And just like that, he deflected her clear, undeniable intuition.

Holly squinted at him, something unreadable flickering in her expression.

From the living room came Maggie's voice: "Why is Precious acting like she's snorted catnip?"

Lily giggled. Holly smirked.

"Come on," Holly said. "Let's go check this out."

They walked out of the kitchen together, curiosity tugging them away.

Brayden exhaled.

Saved from an interrogation, thanks to Precious, he thought, grateful for the feline diversion.

But deep down, he knew…

It was only a matter of time until the cat was officially out of the bag.

Chapter 3

Running the Wrong Program

Redefining the Avatar

Brayden was still standing in the kitchen, half-dazed by Lily's intuitive—and alarmingly accurate—insight, and by how quickly he'd deflected it out of self-protection.

Before he could process it, David entered, snapping him back to reality with yet another costume change. A slight upgrade from his earlier "toilet-cleaning" ensemble, this time David wore a tank top, gym shorts, runners, and the proud smirk of a sixteen-year-old on a mission to sculpt the ultimate beach bod.

David opened the fridge reflexively, scanned it like it might offer life advice, then closed it again.

"Hey Dad, I know you're old and fragile now, but any chance you wanna work out with me? Could be good for your osteoporosis."

Brayden hesitated. His thoughts were still tangled—trailing behind him like loose wires.
But something about David's grin—open, mischievous, genuine—cut through the fog.

He's here. Present. Not scrolling. And he's inviting me into his world for once.

"Yeah," Brayden said, stretching his back. "Why not."

The basement gym smelled like rubber mats, steel, and teenage effort. David started stacking plates, cracking his knuckles like a Marvel character prepping for a fight scene.

Brayden grabbed a dumbbell and eased into a few slow reps.
His body groaned. His shoulders cracked. But it felt good—grounding.
The burn made him hyperaware of his arms. The rhythm of breath and repetition steadied his mind.

And gradually, the chaos in his head began to reorganize itself—like puzzle pieces clicking into place.

The panic attack.
The birthday wish.
The dream.
Craig.
Jake's story.
The bike.
The near miss.
The rage in the field.
The dragonfly.
The stillness.

It was all connected somehow.

Brayden moved to the bench press, inhaling deeply as the barbell lowered to his chest. His breath met the weight. His body met the moment.

A question rose from deep within him:

Who am I, really?

This time, it didn't come as panic. It came as curiosity. Pure, raw, quiet curiosity. Not something to solve.
Something to feel. To experience. To embody.

He glanced at David, who was mid-set, talking like they were at a café.

"I need my license soon. It's getting embarrassing. Ava's little brother drives now. He's like… seven. I don't know. He's small."

Brayden chuckled, exhaling into another curl.

David switched arms. "Also, we need to talk about allowance—and inflation. You can't expect me to buy protein powder and hair gel with the same money you got back in 1856."

Brayden grinned. "I'm in pretty good shape for a 160-something-year-old, don't you think? And see how sharp I still am for calculating that so fast?"

David laughed.

They kept moving—squats, curls, press, repeat.

And as Brayden moved, something inside him began to clarify.

His mind no longer felt like a noisy courtroom.
It felt like a calculator—calm, precise, responsive.
Not a force running him, but a tool he could actually operate in this grounded state.

Maybe this is the way I'm supposed to feel, he thought.
Not checked out. Not escaping. Just here. In the body. In the moment.

And for the first time in days—maybe even years—he wasn't lost in his own stories. It was amazing how simply moving his body could pull him back to his core—out of his agitated mind, and into something solid.

But he could feel something burning inside him.
Quiet, but insistent.
A wild curiosity that refused to be tamed.

Something had been set in motion.
And it wasn't done with him yet.

As he racked his weights and reached for his water bottle, Holly appeared at the top of the stairs.

"Brayden, are you planning on going anywhere later today? I was hoping to get a bottle of white wine to go with dinner tonight."

Brayden wiped the sweat from his brow, heartbeat still steady from the workout.

"Yeah," he said, almost reflexively. "I might head out for a bit."

He smiled at her, but behind the smile… something was shifting.

Because in that moment, he realized:

He had no idea where he'd end up today.
But something told him—
It wouldn't be the liquor store.

The Open Book

Brayden climbed back onto his Harley feeling strong. Clear.
Anchored in his body in a way he hadn't been in a long time.

His muscles ached, but it was a good ache—earned. His breath was deep and steady. The chaotic static that had hijacked his mind earlier was finally giving way to something calmer, more spacious.

To say it had been a strange day was the understatement of a lifetime.

Now, he cruised down the quiet streets of their small town, the early afternoon sun warming his shoulders, the wind in his face.

He figured he'd swing by the liquor store—Holly had asked for a bottle of white to go with dinner.

But somewhere between second gear and the next left turn, his hands moved differently than his mind had planned.

A few minutes later, without any conscious decision, he found himself pulling up in front of *The Open Book*.

The old brick storefront looked exactly the same—weathered, warm, inviting. The hand-painted sign creaked softly in the breeze, its curling script still charming despite the chipped corners.

He parked, removed his helmet, and stepped off the bike like this had always been the plan.
Maybe it had.

A bell tinkled as he pushed open the door.

Inside, the world changed. The scent of old paper and worn leather wrapped around him like a soft memory. Gentle jazz played overhead, blending with the hum of quiet conversation somewhere in the back.

The space hadn't changed. Shelves sagged under the weight of forgotten bestsellers and dog-eared classics. Tables were littered with bookmarks, pencils, and the kind of comfortable silence only found in a bookstore that had survived the rise of Kindle and the fall of attention spans.

Behind the counter stood Jen.

She looked up from a thick hardcover and lit up like someone greeting an old friend.

"Well, well! I had a feeling I'd be seeing you soon," she called, slipping a ribbon into her book. "Long time no see, Brayden. How's life treating you?"

He walked up to the counter, hands in his pockets. "Hey, Jen. I, uh… had a weird experience. And for some reason, I thought of you."

Her eyes sparkled. "Oh, I love weird. Lay it on me."

Brayden leaned on the counter and lowered his voice. "I've been having these thoughts… like maybe I've been living on autopilot. That I've been sleepwalking through a version of life that isn't even mine."

He gestured loosely around him—the books, the street outside, all of it. "I know this sounds nuts, but what if none of this is as solid as it seems?"

Jen's smile widened knowingly. "Ahhh… you've caught the scent of it."

"The scent of what?" he asked.

She leaned in, almost whispering. "Awakening."

He raised a skeptical brow. "You mean… spiritual stuff?"

"Not just spiritual. Scientific too." She turned, reached under the counter, and pulled out a thick tome. *Power vs. Force* by Dr. David Hawkins. It hit the counter with a satisfying thud.

"This one will bend your brain—in a good way. Hawkins was a psychiatrist who mapped out levels of human consciousness. Every emotion, every thought—it's all energy. Measurable. Observable. Transformative."

Brayden tilted his head, intrigued.

Jen grinned and slid over another title: *The Power of Now* by Eckhart Tolle.

"This one'll help you turn down the volume on that narrator in your head."

Just then, Brayden's narrator chimed in, uninvited. *Oh, she knows about the voice in the head?* It was amazing how insidious that little voice was—always sneaking in its commentary while hardly ever being detected.

Then came *Loving What Is* by Byron Katie.

"Question your thoughts, question your suffering. Game changer."

And finally, *The Untethered Soul* by Michael Singer.

"Your blueprint for getting out of your own way."

Brayden stared at the pile. "Jen, I'm an engineer. This is… a lot."

She smiled softly. "You know what else is a lot? Living your whole life not knowing who you really are."

He said nothing. Just looked at the books, his fingers brushing the covers.

His inner voice took over:

Am I standing at the edge of the rabbit hole? Still able to turn back… or already falling in?

The front door creaked open, and a couple walked in. The woman, wrapped in a patterned scarf and exuding cheerful curiosity, gave Jen a wave.

"Hi Nacy! Hi Kevin! Nice to see you again!" Jen called back warmly.

As they passed the counter, the woman spotted a copy of *The Energy Codes* by Dr. Sue Morter on display.

She lit up. "Oh! I loved that one. So powerful. I found a used copy on Craig's List. Lucky me!"

Brayden froze slightly.
Craig's List?

His heart did a little flip. Just a coincidence. Obviously.
But still—the name pulsed like a nudge from somewhere he couldn't see.

Jen turned back to him and tapped the cover of *The Energy Codes* with sudden inspiration.

"You know what? Add this one too. It's a sign from the universe that you need to read it, Brayden."

He gave a shaky laugh. "You're building me a curriculum."

She winked. "Nope. The universe is."

Earlier that morning, lying on the dirt in that field—
the one that had held him through one of his most gut-wrenching moments—

Brayden had wondered how the space inside him, carved open by the purging of old emotions, might ever be filled.

Already, he was starting to get his answer.

The Draw

Brayden was still staring down at the growing pile of books in front of him, wondering what exactly he was getting himself into.
They felt less like reading material and more like coordinates for a spiritual expedition he wasn't sure he'd signed up for.

The engineer in him—the part that never cared for the deeper, more philosophical questions of life—stood at the edge of this moment like it was a cliff.

Jen clapped her hands together. "Oh! I almost forgot! We're holding a draw for a pair of tickets to the Science & Spirituality Conference in Orlando next month. It's a fundraiser for the bookstore. Some of the top speakers in the world are going to be there—Eckhart Tolle, Dr. Sue Morter, Michael Singer… they'll all be presenting. And get this: the prize includes airfare and accommodation."

Brayden raised his eyebrows.

Although "That sounds amazing" were the words that came out of his mouth, his inner voice muttered, *What are you getting yourself into, Brayden? Since when are you into this kind of woo-woo circus?*

Jen continued. "Right? And it's only fifty bucks to enter and support your local bookstore. Totally worth it."

Brayden scratched the back of his neck. "Unfortunately, I never win anything."

Jen's eyes lit up like a switch had been flipped. She leaned across the counter and pointed at his chest.

"No wonder you never win with an attitude like that! Brayden, don't you know you have to *feel* it—like really feel it—and believe it to make it happen? Then you let it go and trust that if it's meant to be, it will. But don't jinx it right from the start!"

He blinked, caught off guard by her intensity. "You sound pretty serious about that."

"Oh, I'm dead serious," she said. "You're walking around collapsing the quantum wave of infinite possibility into a tiny particle of *'I never win anything,'* and then wondering why you don't."

He squinted. "Okay… what?"

Jen grinned. "Alright, science guy, here's the quick version: quantum mechanics. Ever heard of the Heisenberg Uncertainty Principle? Basically, when we observe something—like an electron—it changes. It exists in every possible state until we focus on it. Then boom—it collapses into one outcome."

Still blank.

"Think of your thoughts, beliefs, even your moods like that. They're the observers. If you keep expecting to lose, you're helping that outcome come true. You're focusing your energy on it, locking it in."

Brayden crossed his arms. "So you're saying my belief influences what happens?"

"Exactly. Not some surface-level positive thinking. I'm talking about what you actually believe at the gut level. What you hold in mind is much more likely to manifest. It's not magic. It's focus. Attention. Intention."

Brayden couldn't help laughing. "Okay, fine. Sign me up. I guess I can try expecting something good for once."

Jen beamed and slid the entry form across the counter. "Now *that's* the spirit. Consider the quantum field officially notified."

She reached under the counter and pulled out a small, beautifully carved wooden box. "Write your name and drop it in."

As he scribbled, she gently placed a hand on his shoulder.

"Close your eyes."

He glanced at her. "Seriously?"

"Seriously."

With a sigh, he closed them.

"Now imagine yourself in Orlando. You're at the conference. You see the palm trees, feel the tropical breeze. You walk into the main hall, and there's Eckhart Tolle—live and in person. Feel it. See it. Own it."

Brayden took a breath and let the scene come to life: the buzz of the crowd, the warm air, the sense of something new opening.

Jen's voice softened. "Now… let it go. Trust."

He opened his eyes, feeling slightly ridiculous—but also strangely lighter.

"You really believe in this stuff?"

She winked. "I've seen stranger things, Brayden. Much stranger."

A New Level Unlocked

Brayden looked down at the five books stacked in front of him. He blinked, half-hoping they might disappear if he stared long enough. It was an ambitious pile for someone who used to think yoga was just a stretching scam to sell overpriced mats.

"I think I'll save *Power vs. Force* for another time," he said, eyeing the thick cover. "Not sure my old bones can carry that much spiritual weight all at once."

He glanced toward the door, mildly paranoid that someone from work might walk in and catch him flirting with the mystical. But instead of running, he reached for his wallet.

He tapped the top book, *The Energy Codes*, curiosity tugging at him. "What's this one about?"

Jen lit up like she'd been waiting for that question all day.

"Oh, Brayden—this one ties it all together! You want scientific proof that we're more than just skin and bones? You want to understand how your energy literally shapes your life? Dr. Sue Morter's got you covered."

Brayden opened the cover, flipping through pages of energy field diagrams, chakra illustrations, and nervous system blueprints. It was like someone had merged ancient mysticism with electrical engineering.

His eyes paused on a sketch of cascading fields—like concentric waves of electricity wrapping around the human body. The layout was precise, clean, almost mechanical. He liked that. It made the woo-woo part a little less woo.

Jen leaned across the counter, eyes gleaming. "She explains how we're energetic beings first, and the persona—this body we think we are—is just the housing. And get this: your body? It's a conductor for consciousness."

Brayden blinked. "Like a power cable… for electricity?"

"Exactly!" she said, pointing at him like he'd just passed the midterm.

But before she could say more, the front door opened with a cheerful jingle. A young delivery guy stepped in, holding a bright pink box tied with a ribbon.

"Hey, Jen. Delivery for you."

Jen looked up, surprised. "Me? I didn't order anything…"

He placed the box on the counter, winked, and left with a casual, "Have a sweet day."

She opened it carefully, revealing a selection of bite-sized pastries—mini éclairs, cream puffs, chocolate-covered strawberries, whipped cream towers, and tiny caramel drizzles that looked like they belonged in a museum. On top, a note:

To Jen, from the Biamontes. We love you! Have a great day!

Jen clutched her heart. "Awwww. How sweet—literally!" She beamed at Brayden. "And your timing today is absolutely divine. Help yourself, or I'll likely eat the whole box!"

Brayden laughed. "This just keeps getting weirder. And better."

Jen popped a miniature tart into her mouth and closed her eyes mid-chew.

"Oh my GOD," she moaned dramatically. "This one's got lemon custard. With a brûléed top. Who does that?!"

She reached for another. "Ooh, and this one has caramel and sea salt. Brayden, I think I just tasted enlightenment."

Brayden gingerly picked up a strawberry-filled puff. It was exquisite. Soft, airy, mildly dangerous.

Jen popped another pastry into her mouth and spoke after a slow, blissful, mindful chew. "So, where were we? Ah yes—your existential crisis."

Brayden snorted, brushing crumbs off his jacket. "Keep this between us, alright? I'd rather not get excommunicated from the firm for dabbling in metaphysics."

Jen gave a solemn nod, hand over heart. "Your secret's safe with me. I take pastry-fueled awakenings very seriously."

Her tone softened just slightly. "But seriously, Brayden… that feeling you've had—that sense you've been sleepwalking through someone else's script, like nothing around you is quite real? That's not crazy. That's your real self starting to wake up. *The Energy Codes* just explains the science behind what your gut already knows."

And for a moment, Brayden felt it again—that subtle current running through him. Not anxiety. Not fear. Something electric. Expansive.

Alive.

He slid the final book onto the stack and nodded. "Alright. Let's see where this rabbit hole leads."

As he turned toward the door, Jen called after him, pastry still in hand. "Don't forget, Brayden—you're more than a walking meat suit!"

He grinned. "You're so sweet!"

Jen gave him a whipped-cream smile. "I know, right?"

Brayden stepped outside, the air crisp and cool on his face. He walked to his bike, the bag of books tucked under his arm like top secret material.

As he passed the shop window, he caught a glimpse of his reflection.

And for a second—just a second—he barely recognized himself.

There was something… lighter. Clearer. Like someone had brushed the dust off a part of him he hadn't seen in years.

He strapped the paper bag to the back of his Harley, pulled on his helmet, and kicked the engine to life.

The plan, of course, had been to swing by the liquor store. That was the entire point of the trip.

Instead, he drove straight home—completely unaware that the bottle of white wine had vanished from his mental checklist.

Which would later make him wonder just how much he could actually trust that mind of his.

The Character Upgrade

Brayden pulled into the driveway, the paper bag of newly acquired metaphysical contraband tucked snugly into the Harley's storage compartment like a secret dossier.

He shut off the engine and sat there, staring at the front door like it might open and start judging him.

What the hell am I doing?

He wasn't the kind of guy who bought self-help books—especially not ones featuring chakras, glowing silhouettes, or rainbow-colored diagrams of the human nervous system.
And yet... he couldn't shake the feeling that this was exactly what he needed.

Then—poke.

He flinched so hard he nearly headbutted his own handlebars.

"Didn't mean to scare ya, Brayden. You gotta do something about those nerves!"

He turned.

Oh great. Mow Ron.

That familiar wave of warm irritation surged from his gut to his throat like acid reflux with a personal vendetta.

"I just came by to wish you a happy birthday, bro," Ron said, grinning like he was in a toothpaste commercial. "Saw the big party last night. That banner in your living room? Pretty sure the astronauts saw it from orbit."

Brayden forced a nod. "Thanks."

But Ron, of course, wasn't done.

"Did you see my new baby?"

Brayden squinted. "The Maserati?"

Ron's smile widened. "Yeahhh, buddy. She's a dream. Tell your gorgeous wife she's welcome to take a ride anytime."

He threw in a wink, then strutted back toward his driveway like he'd just dropped a mic.

Brayden blinked.

Did he just—?
Yup. He did. He really just said that.

Instantly, the voice in Brayden's head floored it.

What a jerk. Who says that? TO MY FACE?

His fists clenched. His face flushed. His mind started assembling an imaginary court case.

He took a breath.
Then another.
Then a third.

Nope. Still wanted to punch him.

What came out instead was a dry, weaponized smile.

"I'll see if I remember to pass on the message," he said, followed by a slow-motion eye roll beneath his sunglasses that could've cracked glass.

Ron didn't notice. He was already halfway back to his personal showroom.

Brayden sighed, retrieved the bag from the Harley, and headed up the steps like a man smuggling home a freshly printed alternate identity.

Still simmering.
Still stunned.
But also—somewhere beneath the sarcasm—a tiny ember of awareness flickered.

Old program, he thought.
And kept walking.

As he opened the front door, the warm scent of rosemary and garlic wrapped around him like a bribe.
Holly was humming in the kitchen, something soft and melodic—her happy-cooking hum.

Maybe if he moved fast, he could sneak upstairs and stash the books under the bed.

"I'm back!" he called out casually, trying to pass through like a breeze.

Too late.

Holly peeked around the corner, wooden spoon in hand. Hair tied back, apron on, face glowing from the oven heat.

"Is the wine in there?" she asked, nodding at the bag.

Brayden stiffened. "Oh! Shoot. Uh… I forgot the wine. Sorry."

"Seriously? Then what's in the bag?" she asked, more pointed this time.

"It's nothing. Just… some books."

Her eyes narrowed. "Books? You bought books? Are you okay?"

He laughed nervously and held the bag behind his back. "Just some stuff Jen recommended."

Holly set the spoon down slowly, like she was defusing a bomb. "Oh, *this* I have to see."

"Nah, it's boring. Just engineering stuff. You wouldn't be into it."

"Engineering stuff? You expect me to believe that?"

"Absolutely."

"Let me see."

"Nope."

"Come on…"

"Negative."

Without warning, Holly lunged like a leopard and snatched the bag from his hands.

"Hey!" Brayden shouted, diving after her.

She danced around the counter, laughing wildly, holding the bag high like she'd just stolen his entire life savings.

"What's the big secret? Come on, show me!" she teased.

Brayden lunged. Missed. Lunged again. Missed harder.

At the commotion, all three teens thundered down the stairs like amused spectators entering a cage match.

David, phone in hand, turned on his camera. "What's going on? This looks reel-worthy."

"Dad's got a secret stash of books and won't let me see," Holly declared, waving the bag like a trophy.

Lily crossed her arms, smirking. "Wait—Dad *reads*?"

Brayden pointed. "That's enough from you."

David zoomed in. "What kind of books? Like… actual books?"

"Very funny," Brayden muttered, lunging one last time. But Holly was already at the island.

With the grace of a magician, she dumped the bag's contents across the counter like a dramatic card reveal.

The room fell silent.

Four books stared up at them like a confession:

- *The Power of Now* by Eckhart Tolle
- *Loving What Is* by Byron Katie
- *The Untethered Soul* by Michael Singer
- *The Energy Codes* by Dr. Sue Morter

Even Precious paused mid-grooming to take in the scene.

Holly gasped like she'd just discovered buried treasure. "You… you bought these?"

Brayden scratched the back of his neck, looking like a teenager caught with reality-altering substances. "Yeah… Jen kind of stacked them on me."

There was a pause. Then Holly's eyes lit up.

"These are amazing! Brayden, I read *The Power of Now* years ago! And Byron Katie? Oh my God, she's a genius. And Dr. Sue Morter? You're kidding me. How did you even hear about her?"

Brayden looked genuinely stunned. "I… didn't. It just… happened. You've read these?"

"Not all of them, but I've heard of them," said Holly, now staring at her husband like he was a different species. "You've always said this stuff was nonsense. That if it wasn't measurable, it didn't exist."

He shrugged, lips twitching. "Yeah, well… maybe I'm upgrading the character. Starting to patch some bugs in the system."

They all stared at him—equal parts confusion and mild concern.

Maggie broke the silence. "Huh? Dad, what are you even rambling about?"

David narrated for his video. "Guys, this is what the first stage of midlife crisis looks like."

Holly laughed and wrapped her arms around Brayden from behind, resting her chin on his shoulder. "I don't know what's happening to you… but I like it."

Brayden gave a small nod, unsure of what to say.

Because deep down, something *was* happening.
Something he couldn't explain, didn't understand, and wasn't entirely ready to admit out loud.

But it was too late to pretend nothing had changed.

The download had already started. No privacy. No warning. Just a full system upgrade—right in front of his whole family.

Limitless Potential

Brayden set his new book collection down on the coffee table, almost reverently, then wandered into the dining room. The aroma of roasted vegetables and garlic lingered like a promise in the air. Laughter drifted from the living room—Maggie and David bickering playfully, Lily's soft giggle threading through like music. Holly moved gracefully between stove and table, humming as she laid down the final dishes.

Brayden paused in the doorway, breathing it all in. For once, he felt *here* —not lost in thought, not running a mental checklist. Just… here. If only he could have willed himself into that state last night during his party instead of having a secret monumental breakdown in the bathroom.

"Dinner's ready!" Holly called, her red oven mitts bright against the white dish she carried to the table.

As the family gathered, David stretched like a cat and sank into his chair. "I'm going to savor every bite of this knowing it's Maggie's turn to do dishes."

"Your turn's coming," Maggie shot back. "Probably when there's twice as many dishes as last night's party."

Brayden chuckled, reaching for the mashed potatoes. Holly unfolded her napkin with practiced ease.

Suddenly, Lily winced and dropped her fork, hands flying to her ears.

"What is it, sweetie?" Holly asked, instantly concerned.

Lily squinted. "Another high-pitched tone. You guys really don't hear those? They're like these squealy pressure noises. I get them all the time."

David tilted his head. "Maybe you're part dog. That would explain the shedding."

"Very funny," Lily said with a glare. "Most people can only hear between 20 and 20,000 hertz. That's like... 0.0035% of the total sound spectrum. There's *so* much more sound out there, we just can't hear it."

David sighed dramatically. "She's become a human radio."

"Actually," Lily continued, undeterred, "bats can hear up to 120,000 Hz. Elephants pick up subsonic rumbles. Humans are basically walking around half-deaf."

Brayden raised an eyebrow, impressed. "Where'd you learn all that?"

"I watch science videos while David watches people pop pimples on YouTube."

David grinned. "Hey, that stuff is educational. I know things now. About... pores."

"It's the same with light," Lily added. "We can only see wavelengths between 400 and 700 nanometers. That's another 0.0035% of the electromagnetic spectrum. All the color and light we think is *everything*? It's just this tiny sliver."

David blinked. "So we're basically blind *and* deaf?"

"Pretty much," Lily said with a shrug. "If the full spectrum of sound or light stretched across an Olympic hockey rink, the part humans can detect would be the size of a hockey puck! Maybe smaller."

"Wow," Maggie said, fork mid-air. "That's kinda freaky."

David nodded. "I always knew we were missing something. Like, how do we even know Dad isn't glowing green right now and we just can't see it?"

Lily stabbed a pea with satisfaction. "Finally. A smart comment."

As the others laughed, Brayden chewed slowly, something stirring beneath the surface. A hockey puck on a 60-meter rink. That was all they could sense of reality.

Holly shifted the mood. "Did you have fun at your party last night?" she asked lightly.

Brayden was about to tell her what she wanted to hear when her eyes lit up.

"Oh! I almost forgot… I had the strangest dream." She set her fork down. "Craig was there."

The air tightened.

Brayden froze. His heart skipped. "What did you say?"

Holly's voice softened. "Craig. He was at your party in my dream. Laughing. He was the life of the party."

Maggie tilted her head. "Who's Craig?"

Holly paled. "Oh God," she whispered. "I didn't mean to—"

Brayden's jaw clenched. His eyes locked on hers.

They don't know, Holly.

A heavy silence settled.

"Dad?" Lily asked gently. "Who's Craig?"

Brayden opened his mouth—

But David's phone suddenly lit up on the counter, untouched. A melody burst from the speaker—loud, unmistakable, and completely out of place.

Talking away, I don't know what… what to say, I'll say it anyway…

Not his ringtone. Not even open on any app. Just… playing, uninvited.

"Whoa!" David jumped. "I didn't even touch it!"

Maggie sang along off-key. Lily danced in her chair. Holly tried to shout over the chorus. "Turn it off, David!"

But Brayden wasn't laughing. He stared at the phone, stunned.

Take On Me. A-ha. 1986.

The melody swept through the room like a ghost. It knocked something loose inside him. Something old.

Lily noticed his face. "Dad? Are you okay?"

He tore his eyes away, his voice low. "That was Craig's favorite song. He played it on the drums. Over and over."

"Was Craig your friend?" Lily asked.

Brayden shook his head. Looked her in the eye.

"No. He wasn't my friend." A pause. A breath. "He was my twin brother."

Maggie's fork clattered. "You… have a twin?"

"Had," Brayden said. The word dropped like a stone. "He died when we were fourteen. That song… it was his."

No one moved.

Holly reached for his hand.

He gently pulled away. "That's all I'm going to say about it tonight."

His voice was firm, quiet. Final.

He met each of his children's eyes. "No more questions."

A hush fell over the table. Dinner resumed, but something unspoken had broken the surface.

A fracture. A memory. A door that had been locked for decades had cracked open.

And something—or someone—was stepping through.

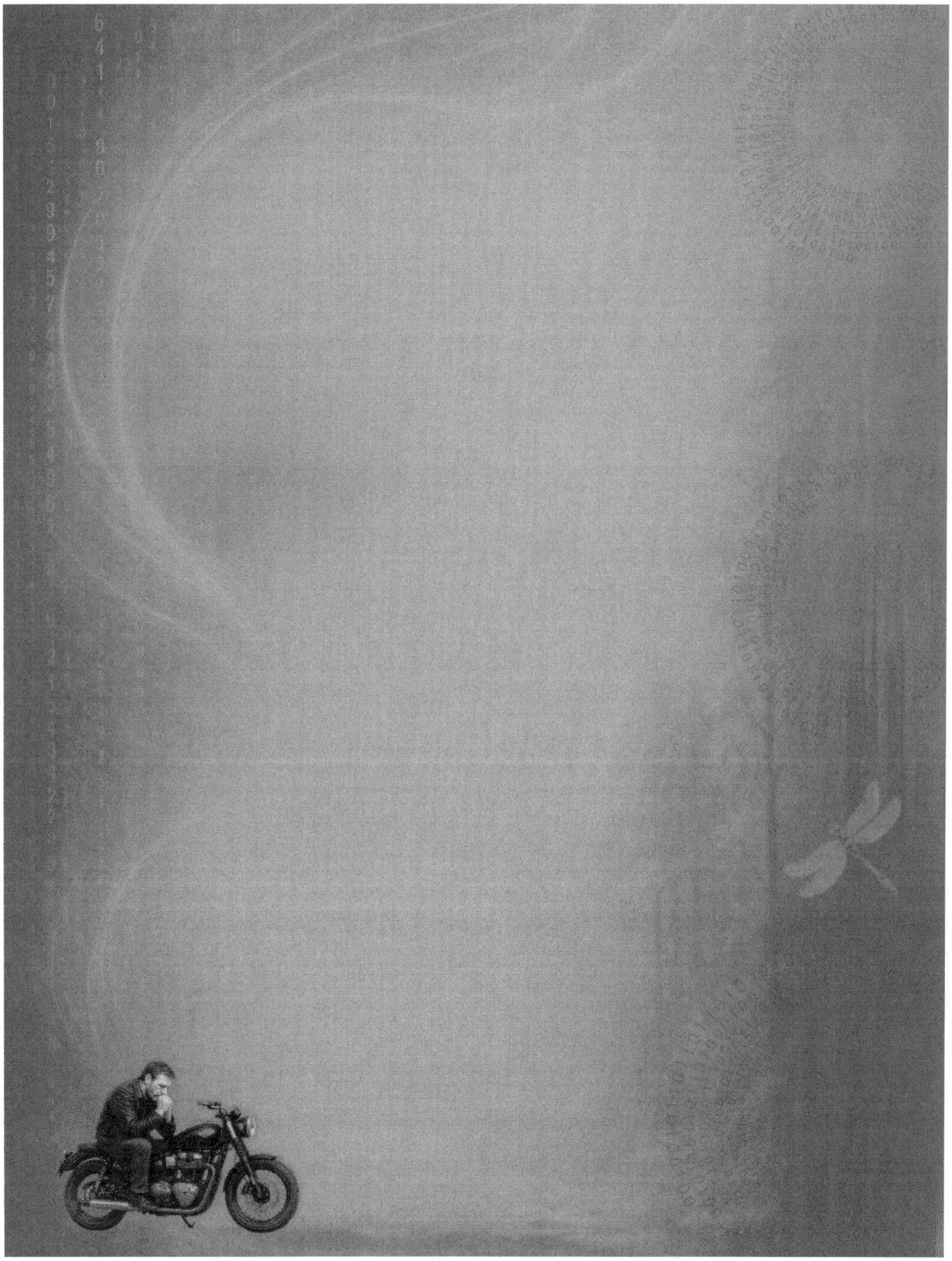

Chapter 4

The Restless Avatar

Secrets Revealed

The bedroom was quiet, bathed in the soft glow of the bedside lamps. Outside, wind whispered through budding branches, and the low call of an owl echoed across the dark fields. Precious lay sprawled between them, purring rhythmically, her warm body rising and falling like a small tide.

Brayden sat upright against the headboard, flipping through *The Energy Codes*, his fingers pausing on each diagram with disbelief and wonder. Was any of this real? And if it was… what did that mean?

Holly shifted beside him, propping herself up on one elbow. "Honey," she began gently, "I'm really sorry I brought up Craig in front of the kids. I forgot it was still something you didn't want to talk about. I should've thought more before opening my mouth."

Brayden didn't answer at first. His eyes stayed fixed on the page, though his mind was miles away—somewhere tangled in memories he had buried decades ago. Finally, he closed the book and looked at her, his gaze heavy.

"It's okay. I know it came from a sincere place."

He hesitated. "But… there's more to the story."

Holly's expression softened. She reached for his hand, wrapping hers gently around it. "What do you mean?"

Brayden exhaled. "Some weird things have been happening. In the last 24 hours. And all of them… they point to Craig."

Holly leaned closer, concern blooming in her eyes. "What happened?"

He took a breath, as though the act of saying it aloud might crack something open again.

"Last night, I had a dream. Craig was in it. He told me, *I'm still here with you. Happy Birthday.* It felt… real, Holly. Vivid. I haven't dreamt of him in years."

She touched his arm. "Brayden… it's your 50th. A huge milestone. Of course you'd think about him. He would've turned fifty too."

"Yeah, maybe," Brayden murmured. "But it didn't stop there. I went to see Jake this morning. I was feeling off. Shaky. When I got there, he was watching a documentary… on near-death experiences."

Holly blinked. "Seriously?"

"Yeah. People who died… and came back with memories of what they saw. I couldn't handle it. I left. Got on my bike. I was just—overwhelmed. Like grief and rage I hadn't touched in decades were clawing their way out."

Holly gripped his hand tighter. "And then?"

Brayden lowered his voice. "Then I heard this voice. Loud. Clear. Not mine. It said, *Pull over, Brayden. Stop.*"

He paused, reliving the moment. Tears welled up. "It was so strong, I couldn't ignore it. So I stopped. Seconds later… two deer sprinted across the road. If I hadn't pulled over…" He trailed off.

Holly gasped, her hand flying to her mouth. "Oh my God… Brayden!"

He nodded slowly. "I parked my bike and just started walking. Into a field. I don't even know why. And then it hit me. All of it. Thirty-six years of grief and guilt and rage. I screamed at the sky, cursed Craig, cursed the universe… I haven't cried like that since I was a kid."

Tears shimmered in Holly's eyes. "That's a good thing… isn't it?"

"Yeah. I guess it is." He looked away, voice soft. "Afterward I collapsed in the dirt. Just lay there, watching clouds drift by like nothing had happened. And then I saw it."

"Saw what?"

"A cloud. Shaped exactly like a dragonfly." He let out a quiet laugh. "I know how that sounds. But it was perfect—the wings, the body, everything."

Holly's eyes widened. "That's actually… really beautiful."

"Craig loved dragonflies. Obsessed over them as a kid. There were dragonflies in my dream last night too." He looked at her, his voice tightening. "And then you tell me you dreamt of him the same night?"

Holly nodded slowly. "I've never dreamt of him before. Not once. And in my dream… he was fifty. Laughing. At peace."

Brayden rubbed his face, his hands trembling slightly. "I don't even know what to say. And then—during dinner—David's phone starts playing *Take On Me* out of nowhere. Craig's favorite song. What are the odds?"

Holly leaned back, watching him closely. "Brayden… I know you don't usually believe in this kind of thing, but… what if Craig is trying to communicate with you?"

Brayden stiffened. He pulled his hand away. "He's been dead for 36 years. When I was a teenager, I begged him for signs. Begged. Got nothing. So why now?"

"Maybe you weren't ready to hear them," Holly said softly. "Grief blocks things. I just watched this internationally renowned medium—Suzanne Giesemann. She used to be a Navy Commander. A total skeptic. Until her stepdaughter died. After that, she started getting signs. Vivid, specific, impossible-to-explain signs. Now she teaches people how to communicate with loved ones who've passed. She says it's like tuning into a radio frequency. But you have to be open."

Brayden opened his mouth to respond, but before he could say a word—

The lights flickered.

Three sharp blinks.

Precious shot upright, staring at something above them, unmoving, her eyes wide.

Holly gasped and instinctively nestled closer. "Oh my God… did you see that?"

"It's just the wind hitting the wires," Brayden said quickly, brushing it off. But his hand trembled slightly on the bedsheet.

He didn't believe in signs. He didn't believe in ghosts.

But his body…

His body told a different story.

A chill ran down his spine. Goosebumps prickled his skin. After 36 years of silence, a long-buried part of him stirred—just enough to let in a whisper he couldn't quite silence:

What if something really had answered his birthday wish?

And what if it had already begun?

Rewriting the Code

Brayden woke with a jolt.

Morning light filtered through the blinds. For a breathless moment, he wasn't anywhere. Just… still. Quiet. Empty.

And then, like a switch being flipped, he was back.

Conscious. Aware. Online.

He lay there blinking, his eyes tracing the shifting patterns of light and shadow above him.

Where was I just now?

He'd never really thought about it before—how he could completely disappear for hours, then be yanked back by sunrise like a puppet on a string. Sure, sometimes he remembered dreams. Glimpses of places and people that felt real while he was in them.

But weren't they just… illusions?

Then again—so is this, he thought suddenly. *What if life is just another kind of dream?*

The thought both thrilled and unsettled him.

Careful not to wake Holly, he slid out of bed and padded into the kitchen, scratching his scalp absently. His body moved on autopilot: scoop the grounds, fill the reservoir, flip the switch. Only when the familiar gurgle began did he snap back into awareness.

I wasn't even here, he realized, shaking his head. *How much of my life is just… programmed?*

The restlessness returned. That low hum under the surface, rising ever since the dream. The voice. The deer.

Coffee in hand, he grabbed *The Energy Codes* and stepped outside.

The backyard glistened with dew. Grass blades sparkled. The air smelled faintly of lilac and pine. He walked to the swing beneath the old oak, its cushions cool from the night. Easing into it, he took a long sip of coffee. The warmth slid down his chest like an anchor.

It felt sacred.

So much had happened in just twenty-four hours.
The dream. The voice. The grief. The dragonfly cloud. Holly's dream. The song. The lights.
And now… this book.

What if I'm more than just this body?

He thought of Jake's documentary. Dr. Eben Alexander's story—brain dead, yet returned with memories. Jake's own experience with his grandmother.

If we're just flesh and bones… how do you explain that?

He had spent his life believing death was the end. Curtain closed. That was it.

But the truth hit him with a strange weight—he'd never actually investigated that belief. He hadn't questioned it. Just… inherited it.

What if I've been wrong this whole time?

A flicker of light caught his eye.

He turned his head—nothing. Just a glint off the bird feeder. Or maybe not even that.

He shook it off.

"Alright, Craig. Or Universe. Or… whatever's out there," he whispered. "I'm gonna open this book five times. Random pages. I'll point to a line. If there's anything you want to show me, now's your chance."

He smiled at the absurdity—but part of him wasn't joking.

First try. Eyes closed. Flip. Point.

"Everything that makes up the entire universe is merely energy in varying wavelengths, vibrating at different frequencies... even physical form is nothing more than compressed energy."

Brayden blinked.

Compressed energy?

His engineer brain perked up—fields, particles, waveforms. If that were true, then matter wasn't solid. And consciousness could… exist beyond it.

He scratched his temple, suddenly aware of how *watched* he felt. Not by a person. By something else. Like reality itself had leaned in.

He glanced behind him.

Still nothing.

Second try. Flip. Point.

"We are energy. Our matter, mind, and thoughts are energy. We are integrated, multidimensional beings made of pure energy. And the degree to which we know this truth about ourselves is the degree to which we live either in pain or bliss."

Multidimensional beings.

It sounded absurd.

And yet… it tugged at something. Like a memory he hadn't made yet.

He glanced down. A diagram: a human figure surrounded by radiant layers.

Physical Body. Etheric Template. Emotional Body. Mental Body. Spiritual Body.

He traced the image slowly. The figure seemed to hum.

Out of the corner of his eye—a flash. Like someone had snapped a photo. He whipped his head around. David pranking him again?

Still nothing.

Okay. I'm either going crazy… or I've got spirit paparazzi.

Third pull. Flip.

"For millennia, spiritual traditions have espoused the notion that we are spiritual beings having an earthly, or physical, experience."

He exhaled.

Spiritual beings… having a physical experience.

The words didn't feel foreign. They felt like something he already knew—but forgot.

Fourth attempt.

"When we really get that everything is energy, including ourselves, we begin to see and exchange with life beneath the physical, material level, on life's subtler levels. Here, we have the greatest power to create a life we truly love."

The subtle levels. Beneath the surface.

He nodded slowly. It was starting to click.

Final try.

"Anything that is happening in the physical body is happening on the energetic level first. Bodily sensations are energy shifts that occur in the energy body and are felt in the physical body."

Brayden froze.

His hand trembled as he closed the book.

And that's when he saw it.

A cardinal.

Bright. Red. Radiant.

Perched on the railing just feet away. Watching him. Still. Unblinking.

His heart thudded.

Did Craig send you… or am I just losing it?

The bird held his gaze for a long, impossible moment.

Then—with a soft flutter—it vanished into the morning light.

Brayden leaned back, eyes tracing the clouds above.

The sky looked different now.

What if I'm more than just this body?

More than he'd ever dared to believe?

But even that question dissolved…

As something deeper rose to the surface:

Not *what's* missing from my life—
But *who?*

Parallel Universes

While Brayden was out in the yard, immersed in a new reality of energy fields, he was completely unaware that his eighteen-year-old daughter was creating a universe of her own—one powered by longing, heartache, and a biochemical cocktail of teenage pheromones pulsing invisibly into the quantum field.

Maggie stirred beneath her covers, eyes still closed, lips curved in a sleepy smile.

She was dreaming of Samuel.

They were walking through a garden, hand in hand, their fingers tangled like they belonged that way. He was wearing that grey hoodie she liked—the one that softened the warmth in his eyes. They paused beneath a magnificent tree, its leaves falling playfully around them. He brushed her soft blonde hair from her cheek, leaned in, and kissed her—gently at first, then deeper, as if the dream itself had breath and heat and want.

She sighed as she drifted upward from sleep.

Half-awake now, she pulled her pillow closer, turned her face toward it, and pressed her lips against the cool cotton like it was his skin.

It wasn't perfect. It was a pillow.
But in her mind, it worked.

She whispered, "God, I hope I see him soon."

Curled beside her, Precious opened one bright green eye and stared knowingly at her human.

The cat didn't make a sound.
But she understood.

Maggie lay there, heart still pounding. Her body tingled in the warm aftermath of the dream, like it had actually happened. Like his hand had really held hers. Like his lips had really found hers.

And that feeling?

It was intoxicating.

Her mind rushed to gather every detail before it vanished—the way he looked at her, the way she felt in his arms, like she was the only girl on Earth who mattered.

It was ridiculous.
And it was everything.

Her thoughts spun like glitter in a snow globe—what if he liked her back? What if he kissed her like that in real life? What if he asked her out?

What if…

She had built a full-on SamuelVerse in her head, complete with backstory, soundtrack, and endless reruns. And it was addictive. The thrill. The fantasy. The longing. It wrapped around her like a warm hoodie that smelled like him.

The desire to be chosen, to be seen, to be someone's favorite person—it ran deep.
It ached.

And it wasn't just about him.
Not really.

It was about what woke up inside her when she thought of him.
The rush.
The hope.
The light.

Precious stretched, yawned, and purred—her whole body vibrating with ease.

She wasn't in love with anyone. She didn't need to be. She purred not to get attention, but because she was content. Because love already flowed through her like a current, asking nothing in return.

If Maggie had been able to hear her speak, she might've said:
Love isn't something you receive. It's something you return to. It's who you are underneath it all.

Perhaps Precious understood how humans go chasing people like medicine, hoping they'll fix the ache, the emptiness, the doubt. And maybe, for a little while, they do. Maybe they make us feel beautiful. Worthy. Special.

But those feelings never last—not if we believe someone else holds the switch.

The truth?

We are the switch.
We are the source.

That pulse Maggie felt in her chest when Samuel kissed her in the dream—that warmth, that softness, that joy—was her own love. Reflected. Amplified. Remembered.

And one day, maybe not today, she'd discover something wild and freeing:

She didn't need someone else to turn it on.

She could flip the switch herself.

And when she did—when she let that love flow from the inside out, not as a need but as a gift to everyone around her—she'd become so magnetic, she might actually need a bodyguard just to keep people from falling at her feet.

But for now?

Romantic love was a rollercoaster. Electric. Dizzying. Addictive. It filled her with nerves and butterflies and impossible hope. And even if she didn't fully understand it yet, she believed—deep in her fluttering chest—that this was what she wanted more than anything in the world.

To be chosen.
To be kissed under a star-filled sky.
To feel whole, safe, and blissfully happy.

But even in the warmth of the dream, her body held a quiet tension—barely noticeable, but there. Her shoulders slightly hunched, her stomach just a little tight. Beneath the glow of imagined love, a familiar current pulsed through her nervous system: the ache of wanting, the fear of not being enough, the pressure to be perfect. Her mind was spinning galaxies of hope—but her body kept the score, responding in ways she couldn't yet name.

Precious stretched again and curled closer, her breath slow and even, like she was synced with something deeper. She didn't need to chase or prove or pretend. She just listened—to the pull of sunlight, the rhythm of breath, the truth in her bones.

Her healing purr and unconditional love quietly communicated:

You have more power over your body than you realize.

You just need to remember how to listen.

Peeking Through the Mirror

While Maggie lay tangled in the dreamy glow of teenage longing, Brayden remained on the swing beneath the old oak, caught in a different kind of trance. His mind was still whirring with the implications of what he'd just read. He set the book aside, stretched his legs, and leaned back. Above him, the branches rustled softly, whispering secrets he couldn't quite hear. A quiet current of energy buzzed just beneath his skin.

Then, a gust of wind swept across the yard, sharp and sudden. His napkin lifted from the table and took flight, flapping like a startled bird before gliding across the lawn. It landed against the base of the weathered shed, resting gently against its chipped frame.

Brayden stood, watching it settle.
Something called him forward.

The shed loomed like a relic from another life. Ivy snaked up the sides like it was being slowly pulled back into the earth.
He rarely went inside.
It was a graveyard of forgotten things—tools, tangled lights, unfinished plans.

He reached for the handle. A ripple of déjà vu passed through him.

The door groaned open, exhaling the smell of wood dust and rust.
He waved a hand through the haze and stepped into the cool dimness.

Light filtered through cracked windows, illuminating particles that hovered mid-air like fairy dust.
And then—he saw it.

The mirror.

Tall. Nearly his height.
Its frame carved with faded, ornate patterns, as though once revered. The glass was flecked with silver and time, its edges blurred like the border of a dream.

He stepped forward, dragging his fingers across the dusty surface.
Clarity streaked through the middle.
And there he was.

Same blue eyes.
Same jaw, softened by age.
Lines along the forehead. Gray threaded through the hair.

He stared into the mirror, and the mirror…
stared back like it knew something he didn't.

His hand touched his cheek. His hair. The crease beside his eye.
But beneath all of it—
There was something that hadn't changed.

A flicker of memory returned:
A boy running wild with Craig.
A teenager, fists clenched, staring at the ceiling in a silent bedroom.
A man at his wedding, laughing with eyes full of light.

And behind every version of him—
That same quiet observer.

He leaned in and whispered to the reflection:
"Who are you really, Brayden?"

No echo. Just stillness thick as fog.

It didn't feel like a mirror anymore.
It felt like… a window.

His breath slowed. His chest softened.

And then—it clicked.
Not as a thought.
But as a knowing.

I'm not the body.
I'm the one who sees the body change…
but doesn't change.

A soft peace washed over him.
Shoulders dropped. Jaw relaxed.

He laughed—quiet, sudden, like someone who had just solved a riddle only the universe could've written.

What watches the body grow older,
but never ages?

He didn't need the answer.
He could feel it.

That presence behind his eyes.
Still. Steady.
Still… him.

He lifted his hand from the mirror, leaving faint streaks behind—like the fingerprints of a ghost remembering it had hands.

And then—

BWAAAAAAAHHHH!!!

The shriek of an engine shattered the silence like a jackhammer in a library. Brayden flinched so hard, he nearly knocked over a bucket of nails.

Mow Ron.
Of course. His next-door neighbor and self-appointed lawn sheriff.

There he was—7:42 a.m. sharp—mowing with military precision, shirtless and oblivious, zigzagging over a perfectly trimmed lawn with the intensity of a Formula 1 pit crew.

The sacred moment had officially been run over.

Brayden let out a breath somewhere between a sigh and a snort.
"Well… peace was nice while it lasted."

He turned away from the mirror, brushing sawdust from his sleeves—and that's when he saw it.

A plastic tote against the far wall.
Faded label: Old Photo Albums—his own handwriting, crooked and worn.

He blinked.

He hadn't touched those in years.

The same magnetic pull that had brought him to the mirror nudged him forward again. He lifted the tote onto the workbench, a cloud of dust rising like old breath.

Inside:
Leather-bound albums, cracked and curling at the edges.
Memories waiting in the dark.

His hand hovered over the thickest one. Faded green cover. Gold lettering nearly gone.

The album.

He hadn't opened it since…

God. Since before he left home.

He paused.

Held it.

Felt the weight of everything it might hold.

Then he turned toward the house.
Steps light.
Mind open.

Suddenly—barking. Close. Getting closer.

"Not again," Brayden muttered.

Mow Ron's dog. Of course.

The pit bull had a legendary talent for chasing squirrels, Amazon drivers, and occasionally his own tail in homicidal circles. If Mow Ron actually kept him on a leash like he was supposed to, maybe the beast wouldn't go barreling through the neighborhood like a grenade with legs and no safety pin.

Brayden set the photo album down and walked to the front of the house, bracing for impact.

The Price of Silence

Moments ago, Brayden had been serene—centered in his breath, grounded in stillness, wide open to life.
And now?
Now it felt like someone had dropped a defibrillator on his nervous system.

The barking was back.
And with it, a jolt so sharp it shattered his inner stillness like glass on concrete.
From calm lake to crashing ocean in half a heartbeat.

His chest tightened. Jaw locked.
Shoulders, which had just hung loose and light, were suddenly welded into place by an invisible armor.
Every muscle braced for impact.

"For a lawyer," Brayden thought, "the guy sure doesn't have much respect for the law."

He rounded the corner just in time to see LeBron—a muscular pit bull with a taste for chaos—tearing across the lawn like a rogue linebacker in a fur coat, tongue flapping, eyes wild with squirrel-chasing glory.

Brayden muttered, "LeBron. Honestly. Who names a pit bull LeBron?"

He pointed with quiet authority. "Go home."

LeBron skidded, spun in a sheepish circle, then darted back toward his own yard. He knew the drill.
And so did Brayden.

Because right on cue, the sputter of a riding mower cut out, and a voice thundered toward the garage like a sitcom entrance:

"LeBroooon! You absolute delinquent! You're gonna get Daddy locked up. No rotisserie chicken for you tonight, baby!"

Fifty-five years old, tanned like a saddle, wearing a black tank top two sizes too small—strategically chosen to show off biceps the size of boulders sculpted by ego.

He grabbed the leash hanging beside the workbench and clipped it to the dog's collar, chuckling like this daily drama was just part of his larger-than-life charm.

Brayden took a deep breath. This time, he'd say something.
He wasn't going to get bulldozed by Ron's energy again.

"You know, Ron, you really need to—"

"Brayden, my man!" Ron boomed, cutting him off with the precision of a courtroom objection. "Hang tight."

Still gripping LeBron's leash, he strutted over, pulling two crumpled tickets from the zip pocket of his gym shorts.

"Oilers game. Center ice. Next weekend," he said, handing them over like a peace offering wrapped in testosterone.
"Can't go. Taking my new girlfriend Kiki to Paris. She's a ten. Yoga instructor. You know the type—flexible morals and hamstrings. I told her, if you keep stretching like that, I might just marry you on top of the Eiffel Tower."

He laughed at his own joke.

Brayden blinked. "Uh… thanks?"

"No worries, brother." Ron tied the leash to a beam inside the garage.
"Three divorces and I finally get it—keep 'em pampered, keep 'em loyal. Spa resort just outside Versailles. You should see the size of the hot tub."

He kept going. Brayden tried to follow.
Something about golf scores. A new condo. An investment in cryotherapy pods. An ice bath he swore boosted testosterone and upgraded his nervous system.

"Cold plunges, man. Shrinks the blood vessels, expands the confidence. You haven't lived till your parts go numb at 5 a.m."

Brayden nodded. Or maybe twitched. It was hard to tell anymore.

Ron checked his watch.
"Alright, bro. Gotta finish mowing before the sun starts flexing. I should come do your lawn sometime. No offense, but it's starting to look like a chia pet's bad side. Catch you later!"

He leapt onto the mower, fired it up like a jet engine, and disappeared behind the hedge—leaving behind a cloud of cologne and exhaust.

Brayden stood there, holding the tickets, trying to locate his spine.
He had gone outside to assert a boundary.

And now?
He was holding center-ice seats to the Oilers game.

The issue was gone.
Neatly defused.

He let out a long, slow breath.
Silenced by sports tickets.

It was such an easy strategy, wasn't it?
Distract. Reward. Redirect.
Bury the tension beneath convenience and charm.

He couldn't help but wonder—how many times in this world were people silenced not by force, but by covert manipulation?
By charisma. By flattery.
By calculated gestures engineered to tug the strings of human wiring—craving, guilt, approval, shame.

It hit him with uncomfortable clarity:
Our default programming makes us vulnerable.
Predictable.
Easy to manage.

And those who understand that—consciously or not—often run the show.

He looked down at the tickets in his hand.
Still warm.

There was so much to wake up from.

And not all of it looked like a nightmare.
Some of it looked like kindness. Or friendship.
Or casual neighborly goodwill.

But beneath it?
Still the game.
Still the code.

He turned back toward the swing beneath the old oak—where the photo album lay in quiet invitation, waiting for him to remember how the programming of his life had been installed, one page at a time.

Programming Revealed

Brayden sat cross-legged on the living room floor, the photo album resting in front of him like an unopened time capsule. The house was still quiet—no clatter from the kitchen, no footsteps overhead. Just the soft morning light pressing through the curtains and the slow return of his breath to normal.

He ran a hand across the worn leather cover, pausing for a moment before peeling it open. It was strange how the body could hold onto tension, even when the threat was gone. His jaw was still tight. His shoulders still humming from the energetic whiplash of his encounter with Ron.

Mow Ron.

Master of the conversational hijack. King of unsolicited bicep flexes and psychological curveballs.
One minute, Brayden had been preparing to set a boundary.
The next, he was holding center-ice Oilers tickets like a confused contestant on a game show.

But that was the thing about programming.
You didn't always see it while it was happening.
You just reacted—automatically, obediently—like a well-trained avatar responding to a system it didn't even know it was part of.

Brayden exhaled slowly, letting the hum settle, and turned the first page.

There they were.

He and Craig—maybe eight or nine—splashing around in the creek behind their childhood home, water swirling around their ankles. Both boys beamed with wild, unfiltered joy. Craig clutched a fishing rod made of sticks and string, his soaked shirt clinging to him like a badge of adventure.

Brayden smiled softly, brushing his thumb across Craig's face. The memory returned with vivid texture and sound—the splash of water, the smell of moss and bark, the way their laughter rang through the trees like wind chimes.

He turned the page.

There they were again—racing bikes down the dirt path, dust clouds swirling in their wake. Then climbing the old oak tree, legs dangling from thick branches, faces tilted to the sky.

They were always running.
Always laughing.
Always just… being.

His chest swelled with something tender and bittersweet.

I remember that feeling.

Life had no sharp edges then. No roles to perform. No masks to wear.

He and Craig had simply existed—wide open, fully alive, as if joy was their natural language.

Another page.

Christmas morning. Matching flannel pajamas. Grins stretched from ear to ear as they tore through wrapping paper. Their mom stood off to the side, smiling faintly, a beer bottle in one hand.

She'd been happy that year.

The darker days came later—when Dad couldn't find work and survival started warping her voice into something louder, sharper.

Brayden stared at the photo. These weren't just frozen images.

They were windows.
Glimpses of freedom, caught mid-breath.
No fog. No second-guessing. Just wonder, presence, and raw delight.

He lingered there for a while, letting the warmth of it wash through him.

Then—he turned the page.

And the innocence shifted.

Twelve. Then thirteen. The smile tighter now. The shoulders more guarded.

The light in his eyes still flickered—but something else had arrived.
Something quieter.
Heavier.

He paused at a photo outside the school gym—hands buried in his pockets, smile stiff.

He remembered that day.
The school dance.
The anxiety.
The unbearable pressure to fit in.

What if they don't like me? What if I say the wrong thing? What if I'm not enough?

He had buried those thoughts.

But they hadn't disappeared.
They had taken root.

He turned the page.

Hockey team photo. He was laughing with the others—but he remembered the pressure. The shame of missing a shot. The sick twist in his gut when he did.

I'll mess it up. I don't belong. I'm not strong enough.

At first, they were just whispers.

But over time, they became grooves.
Well-worn mental paths, walked daily, unquestioned.

They didn't feel like thoughts anymore.
They felt like truth.

His hands trembled slightly as he flipped again.

His teenage self stared back—eyes distant, posture tight.

Brayden could still feel it in his body.
The knots in his chest.
The restlessness in his limbs.
The quiet fear of never being enough.

He rubbed his sternum absentmindedly, tracing the phantom ache still lodged deep inside.

How much of my life has been shaped by these invisible stories?

Clarity was rising now—cutting through the haze.

This is how it happened, he realized.

From barefoot in the grass to walking school hallways with his eyes fixed on the floor.

It hadn't come all at once.
It had crept in.

Beliefs. Fears. Doubts.

They had wrapped themselves around his nervous system like ivy—silent and persistent—until he couldn't tell where the programming ended and he began.

Somewhere in those pages, he saw the moment it started:

The quiet disappearing act of his real self.

To stay safe, to be accepted, to be loved—he had learned to morph. To become what others needed.

A helper. A pleaser. An achiever. A shield.

Strong. Polite. Reliable.

Never too loud.
Never too sad.

But now…

Now he could see it.

The truth rose inside him like a tide:

It wasn't real.
It wasn't him.

It was a survival system.

A brilliant piece of code, written in childhood, to navigate a world that didn't always feel safe. Just… programming.

And now that he'd seen it—really seen it—he couldn't go back.

The question surfaced like smoke from an old fire:

Could it be rewritten?
Could he delete the fear-based software?
Could he finally live from the deeper truth inside him—beneath the layers, beneath the armor?

He didn't know.

Not yet.

But something in him whispered:

Yes.

Chapter 5

Initiating Override Mode

Removing the Mask

Brayden was still on the living room floor, the photo album lying open before him like an artifact from another life. But he wasn't looking at the pictures anymore.
He had seen something.
Felt something.
And now it was rising.

The past hadn't just given him memories—it had exposed the exact moment he began to disappear. The moment the real him—the vibrant, openhearted boy with nothing to prove—started fading behind masks he didn't even know he was wearing.

He had seen the code behind the curtain.
Felt the glitch ripple through his system.
And now, the awareness was rising.
And it couldn't be buried again.

Now… he could see the programming.
Not metaphorically. Literally.
A set of coded beliefs, written early, running his system without question.

And something inside him stirred—not with grief, but with possibility.
He could rewrite it.

He sat up straighter, energy building in his chest. Not adrenaline—something steadier. Truer.
He looked up—and noticed Precious casually strolling into the living room, heading straight for the bright window ledge, completely unbothered by his existential breakthrough.

"Precious," he said, rubbing his temple, "do you think I can actually rewrite the code? You know… the programming?"

She looked at him and meowed once, unimpressed.

"At least you're not plagued by some voice in your head. You've got instincts, sure—but no inner monologue harassing you every five seconds, right?"

She blinked slowly. Like she'd already transcended such nonsense.

He chuckled, pushed himself off the floor, and grabbed his notebook from the coffee table. Flopping onto the couch like a man on a mission, he clicked his pen. A fresh page flipped.

Although he hadn't made it past chapter two in any of his new books, what was coming through now didn't feel like learning—it felt like remembering.

At the top of the page, he scrawled:

The Real Me vs. The Program

And then:

The Default Program (a.k.a. The Avatar):
• Reacts to every thought like it's true
• Runs on autopilot, unaware of the moment
• Lives in the mind—analyzing, judging, planning
• Bottles up emotions, avoids feeling
• Sees life as a struggle, always striving
• Wants more—money, time, validation
• Tries to control everything to feel safe

He glanced at Precious again. "You've got your survival code too, huh?"

She remained curled up, a living shrug.

"Yet somehow, you're still more peaceful than ninety percent of humans."

He shook his head with a grin and flipped to a clean page.

The Real Me (a.k.a. The Player):
• Observes thoughts instead of obeying them
• Lives in the body, rooted in the now
• Feels everything—without judgment
• Knows emotions are energy, not identity
• Doesn't need more to be whole
• Trusts life instead of trying to control it

He leaned back and stared at the two lists.
Two identities.
Two operating systems.
One tight and reactive. The other fluid. Free.

"So," he murmured, "which one have I been running?"
He laughed out loud.
The answer wasn't exactly subtle.

Still, something in him wanted a metaphor.
Something that would stick.
Something he couldn't forget the next time the old code tried to boot back up.

He flipped to a fresh page and wrote furiously for a few minutes:

Avatar vs. Player (Mind vs. Body)

Then, standing up with sudden theatrical energy, he turned toward Precious like she was his personal Broadway audience.

"Oh, you're gonna love this," he said.

She raised her head with the faintest look of suspicion.

He cleared his throat and prepared to launch into a full-body performance—half poem, half spoken-word musical, completely ridiculous.
As if he needed to prove to himself that he *could* snap out of the programming… simply by doing something wildly out of character.

Avatar vs. Player

The Avatar—it thinks nonstop,
Obsessed with time, the ticking clock.
Stuck in the past or fearing tomorrow,
Drenched in doubt or steeped in sorrow.

It feeds on fear, it loops with dread,
It lives in stories in my head.
It needs control, it grips with might—
It'd rather die than not be right.

Dear Avatar, you're not what's real.
You sure can think—but cannot feel.
You are the mind. You are the code.
But you can't live on silent mode.

As for the Player? A different game.
No need to prove, no thirst for fame.
It breathes, it feels, it moves with grace,
It meets the moment face-to-face.

It trusts, it flows, it's calm inside—
No fear to run from, none to hide.
It doesn't posture, push, or strive—
It knows it's built to bloom and thrive.

It smiles, it sings, it leaps, it plays,
It greets the world with love and praise.
It knows itself—clear, bold, and strong…
I've had its power all along.

He reached the final line of the poem and—unable to help himself—threw his arms wide and belted it out at the top of his lungs:

"I'VE HAD ITS POWER ALL ALONG!"

The note landed somewhere between a war cry and a foghorn.

Precious winced. Her ears pulled back in visible protest.

He glanced at her mid-pose. "Too much?"

She turned her head away, looking offended.

He finished with an exaggerated bow. Precious blinked. Then yawned.

"Harsh critic," Brayden said, grinning.

He collapsed back onto the couch, catching his breath. He hadn't felt this alive in years.

Then—a giggle.

He turned.

David stood in the doorway, phone in hand, grinning like he'd just hit the jackpot.

"Dad… were you just having a *Broadway moment* with the cat?"

Brayden sat up straighter. "It was performance art."

David raised the phone. "Captured in 4K."

Brayden's eyes widened. "Don't you dare."

"I'm sending it to Maggie."

"You little punk. Get back here!"

David squealed and bolted. "TikTok needs to see this new musical genre!"

Brayden shot off the couch, nearly tripping over his own feet. "The world is *not* ready!"

They thundered down the hallway, two generations of mischief, roaring with laughter. Brayden finally stopped at the base of the stairs, breathless and beaming.

His ribs ached. His cheeks hurt. His chest was light.

And above him, David's laughter spilled out like sunlight.

Brayden, still catching his breath, reached into his hoodie pocket and pulled out a folded pair of hockey tickets.

"Man," he called up casually, just loud enough to be heard, "I don't know who I'm going to invite to the Oilers game next weekend. Center ice seats. Maybe Jake wants to go with me."

Sudden silence. Then—

"Wait—*what!?* You got center-ice tickets for the Oilers?!"

Brayden smirked. "Yep. Dead center. Perfect view."

David reappeared at the top of the stairs in a flash. "I would do *anything* to go to that game! I'll delete the video—I swear!"

Brayden tucked the tickets back into his pocket and gave a slow, theatrical wink.

"I'll think about it."

A Fresh Perspective

Brayden was still catching his breath from chasing David when Holly shuffled into the kitchen, wrapped in her flannel housecoat, hair tousled like she'd just lost a wrestling match with her pillow.

She squinted at him. "What on earth is going on? Was that you singing—or some cat in heat?"

He wiped his flushed face with both hands. "Oh… long story. Just had to bribe your son, who threatened to make me famous with my new song. Luckily, Ron gave me two Oilers tickets this morning. That was enough leverage for Dave to delete the video."

Holly yawned, reaching into the fridge for strawberries and blueberries. "Teenagers and phones. A dangerous combo. But I *want* to see that video before he deletes it! It sounded like quite the performance."

Brayden grinned, gave her shoulder a light squeeze, and wandered back into the living room.

The morning sun had stretched across the floor now, illuminating the old photo album still lying open like a portal.

He sat down and turned the page, still buzzing from his spontaneous musical debut. The sprint after David had acted like an accidental HIIT workout, flooding his body with energy and good hormones.

But the moment his eyes landed on the next photo, the charge shifted. Little arrows of deeply buried pain pierced straight through his chest.

And there it was.

A picture of him and Craig, snapped just a week before the accident. Rogue, their scruffy mutt, bounded between them, tongue lolling, tail a blur. The boys were beaming, chasing each other through golden fields. Mischief in their eyes. Life at full volume.

Brayden swallowed hard.
They'd had no idea.
That day had felt so ordinary.
Perfectly, heartbreakingly ordinary.

He turned another page.

Craig's funeral.

The memory struck like a wave—tight throat, heavy chest, his mother's trembling hand clamped around his arm. Her perfume mixed with alcohol. The lilies. The hush.

But then… something else.

Above Craig's casket, just beneath the stained-glass window: a strange, glowing circle of light. Small. Translucent. Edged with gold.

His brow furrowed.
Camera flare?

He leaned in closer. It hovered just over Craig's shoulder. Too perfect. Too precise.

He reached out and touched the photo.
A whisper of light, like something trying to be seen.

His heart thudded.

A few minutes later, Holly walked in, cradling a plate of fruit and warm croissants.

"Breakfast, courtesy of your adoring wife," she announced.

"Thanks, babe."

She sat beside him, eyes twinkling. "What are you looking at?"

He rotated the album toward her. "This."

She leaned in. "Oh… wow." Her finger hovered over the light. "You never noticed that before?"

He shook his head slowly. "Not once."

"I've heard people say those are spirit orbs," she murmured. "You know… energy."

Brayden chuckled under his breath. "Yeah… maybe."

But she was already flipping the page.

And there it was—his fifteenth birthday. Just months after the funeral. A small cake. Fewer people. Candles burning too bright. Everyone trying too hard to smile.

She leaned closer, eyes narrowing. "Look," she whispered, pointing to the window behind him.

Brayden's heart stumbled.

There, faint in the glass… a reflection. A boy's face. Craig's face. Pale. Gentle. Like mist caught on film.

He froze. "How… how did I not see that? It looks like it was photoshopped."

"Maybe," Holly said softly, "you weren't ready to."

Brayden turned the page again, his pulse quickening.

A family photo—just him and his parents at some dull holiday gathering. He could still feel the emotional flatness from that day.

But something new caught his eye.

Pinned to his jacket: a tiny dragonfly brooch.

His breath caught. "No way…"

"What is it?" Holly asked.

He shook his head, dazed. "I found that pin on the sidewalk. The morning after I dreamed of Craig. I picked it up and wore it. I never thought it meant anything."

Her hand gently rested on his. "And now?"

Now… everything felt different.

He didn't answer. Words would only dilute it.

The moment held its breath.

Maybe he had never seen these things before… because he hadn't been *looking*.
Not really.
Not with an open mind.

He'd always dismissed signs as coincidence. Magic as wishful thinking. Spirit as a crutch for the weak.

But how could you find something you didn't believe existed?

If you never revisit the crime scene…
You miss the evidence hiding in plain sight.

His fingers lingered on the dragonfly pin. His eyes returned to the photo.

A new question whispered in the silence:
What else have I missed?

He was about to speak when the sound of footsteps thundered above.

"Mom! Dad!"

It was Lily—her voice sharp with panic.

They both bolted upright.

"Maggie just threw up—and she has a fever!"

Brayden's heart plummeted.

Holly gasped and ran. "Coming, sweetheart!"

Brayden stood there, frozen, the album still open before him.

The orb. The face. The pin.

The signs.
The synchronicities.

The dragonfly gleamed faintly in the light as upstairs, the world shifted again.

And deep in his bones, he could feel it—
Something was being asked of him now.

Something he wasn't sure he was ready for.

But the invitation was clear.

Would he answer?

Overcoming Obstacles

Brayden stood frozen in the hallway, Lily's alarmed voice still echoing in his ears.

Not again.

He shook himself out of it and hurried upstairs, heart pounding against his ribs. Maggie's faint groans drifted down the hall—thin, strained, and all too familiar.

He stepped into her room.

Holly was already at her side, pressing a cool cloth to Maggie's forehead, her movements calm and focused in that quiet, instinctive way only a mother's could be. Maggie lay curled on her side, arms wrapped around her middle, her skin pale and slick with sweat.

Brayden hovered in the doorway, helplessness washing over him like a tide.

He'd seen this scene before.
Too many times.

Fevers. Fatigue. Weeks of aching limbs. The same pattern, repeating like clockwork. The doctors called it chronic fatigue syndrome. Others hinted at stress, or some elusive immune condition.

But Brayden had always sensed something deeper—something no one else seemed willing to look for.

He remembered what Holly had told him months ago, her voice taut with worry:
It all started when she was fifteen.

The year Maggie's anxiety began to take shape.
When her natural brightness turned sharp-edged.
When getting straight A's became a source of panic.
When looking perfect meant hours in front of the mirror and skipped meals.
When friendships started to feel like competitions.

"She was fine last night," Holly whispered, glancing up at him with red-rimmed eyes. "Just tired. Then this…"

Brayden stepped closer and gently placed a hand on Maggie's damp forehead. Her skin was hot—too hot. Her eyelids fluttered open at his touch.

"Hey, sweetheart," he said softly. "Rough morning, huh?"

She gave a faint, sleepy smile. "Samuel… it's happening again," she murmured.

Brayden's stomach twisted.

Her cheeks were flushed, her skin clammy—she was burning up. And in her fevered haze, she thought Samuel was there beside her.

But it wasn't just her body crashing. It was the whole spiral that came with it—the tests, the missed classes, the specialists who offered theories but no answers. The quiet shame that settled in when her body wouldn't cooperate.

But this time… Brayden saw it differently.

He thought of the notes he'd scribbled that morning. The Player versus the Avatar. Survival mode, running like background code. The mind, spinning with *shoulds* and fears and pressure to perform.

Wasn't that exactly where Maggie was stuck?

Trapped in overdrive.
Trying to prove her worth in a world that had taught her not to rest.
Not to soften.
Not to *be*.

"Try to rest, honey," Holly whispered, brushing the hair back from Maggie's forehead. "We've got you."

Maggie nodded weakly, her lashes already falling shut.

Brayden lingered for a moment, then followed Holly into the hallway and gently closed the door behind them.

"It's happening more often," he said quietly.

"I know." Holly leaned against the wall, her face drawn. "She's only eighteen, Brayden. She should be out with friends. Laughing. Dating. Living her life. Not… this."

He rubbed her shoulder. "We'll figure it out. I promise."

But even as he said it, a familiar ache bloomed in his chest—the ache of knowing he couldn't fix this with reassurance alone.

His thoughts turned to *The Energy Codes*. He hadn't finished the book, but the ideas had planted themselves like seeds.

Emotions are energy.
They don't disappear just because we ignore them.
They lodge in the body. The muscles. The tissues that never fully let go.
They block the current. Disrupt the flow. Dim the spark.

He remembered the diagram—seven chakras aligned down the spine, a vertical current running through the center, connecting above and below.

It had felt radical. Like a foreign language.
Yet something in it rang true.

What if Maggie's illness wasn't just physical?

What if her body was reflecting everything her mind had absorbed?
The fear of failure.
The perfectionism.
The belief that she had to earn love through excellence.

But how do you say that to your daughter?

How do you tell her that maybe—just maybe—her healing won't come from another supplement, another specialist, another label?

That maybe, it begins by feeling what she's been trying so hard to suppress?

Brayden wasn't sure she could hear that yet.
He wasn't even sure he was ready to say it.

"Maybe we call Dr. Fisher again," Holly said. "There might be something new he can try."

Brayden nodded slowly. "Yeah. Maybe."

But his thoughts were elsewhere.
Deeper.

A truth hummed beneath the surface, quiet and persistent—like a frequency just beyond hearing.

The next test isn't the answer, the knowing whispered.
The next diagnosis won't bring peace.

He looked back toward Maggie's room, listening to the soft rhythm of her breath.

Something in her system was trying to speak.

And for once, Brayden felt like maybe—just maybe—he was beginning to understand the language.

Not one of symptoms or prescriptions.

But of energy.
Emotion.
Belief.

What if healing didn't come from outside at all?

What if the key wasn't in fixing the body…
but in finally feeling what the body had never been allowed to release?

What if that energy field—strange as it seemed—was real?
And what if Maggie could learn to embody it?

Unplugging Initiated

Weeks went by—work, home, repeat—but something was loosening beneath the routine.

Brayden still suited up each morning: tailored navy wool, hand-stitched cuffs, Italian silk lining. His leather shoes gleamed like polished obsidian. His watch—an artifact from a long-forgotten promotion—glinted with quiet authority. The kind that said, *I've made it,* without needing to shout.

His BMW waited in the garage. Coffee steamed in the cupholder. The same playlist queued up on the drive to work.

But now, the passenger seat was always stacked with books: *The Energy Codes, The Power of Now, Loving What Is, The Untethered Soul.* His new sidekicks.

One morning, he caught his reflection in the side mirror—slick, professional, composed.

The Avatar, he thought. *Playing the part.*

It wasn't wrong, necessarily. Just... automatic.

And for the first time, he wasn't sure he wanted to keep playing.

Subtle shifts crept in.

He began waking earlier—before the footsteps overhead. Sometimes he'd sit with coffee and silence. No to-do list. No mental dress rehearsal. Just breath, warmth, and stillness.

Strangely, that began to feel like everything.

Throughout the day, he'd pause.

Am I here right now?

Tension in the jaw? Shoulders?
Breathe into it.

These micro-moments—barely noticeable—were like tugging loose threads from a tightly woven sweater. His programming began to fray.

Even work felt different.

He still delivered. Still hit deadlines. Still played the part of the capable, competent engineer. But now he noticed things—things that had always been there, hiding just beneath the surface.

The tight smiles in meetings. The careful phrasing. The subtle power plays dressed up as collaboration. The status games disguised as "professionalism."

It was like watching a well-rehearsed play. Every character sticking to their lines. Every scene performed on cue.

And he'd been one of them.

Running the script, he thought. *Without even realizing it.*

He noticed it at Friday poker nights too—his old crew from university, still going strong. But now, the whole performance glared like stage lights.

The cigars.
The bravado.
The inside jokes.
The subtle digs.
The overcompensating laughter.

The Masculinity Mask, he called it. Worn by all, questioned by none.

He still showed up. Still shuffled, still dealt. But something in him had already folded. It felt like dressing up for a role he no longer auditioned for.

What began replacing those rituals was something entirely different.

On the way home from work, he'd take detours—off the main roads, away from the lights and noise. He let instinct guide him more than GPS, eventually discovering a break in the trees just off the highway.

His secret haven.

A wild clearing where the forest opened just wide enough to let sunlight spill in like holy light. He'd park beneath the whispering branches, grab a notebook… or simply vanish.

No signal.
No performance.
No mask.

Just trees.
Wind.
Breath.
Earth.

Sometimes he'd sit cross-legged in the grass, eyes closed, spine against a warm rock. Other times, he watched ants navigate mossy stones or traced the way light flickered through the leaves until thought gave way to presence.

Once, he lay flat on the forest floor, palms pressed to the dirt, and thought: *This is what coming home feels like.*

In nature, the energy was different. Calmer. Truer.
It didn't rush.
It didn't posture.
It didn't ask him to be anything but there.

It just *was.*

And somehow, being near that kind of presence helped him remember his own.

But not everyone celebrated his new rituals.

He started coming home later—sometimes after dinner, after the dishes were rinsed and the house had dimmed.

At first, Holly gave him space.

But space eventually became suspicion.

Tight lips. Half-asked questions.

"Did you forget what time it was?"

"I lost track," he'd say.

"Well maybe you should start tracking again."

Some nights, she waited up for him—book unopened in her lap, TV murmuring in the background. She'd ask where he'd been. What he was doing.

"Thinking. Processing," he'd offer, vague but sincere.

She'd nod. But her eyes asked something else:

Who are you becoming?
And why are you leaving me behind?

The kids noticed too.

Maggie's health still swung between bursts of energy and invisible crashes. Her face would brighten for a moment, only to dim again under the weight of fatigue and the anxiety she worked so hard to hide.

David had grown more distant—buried in his phone, endlessly scrolling. His mood seemed tethered to the algorithm—higher with every like, lower with every silence.

And Lily? She had grown quieter than ever. Shoulders hunched. Eyes skimming past mirrors. Secretly comparing herself to the prettier, more popular, more effortlessly perfect girls on Instagram—the ones who seemed to float through life in curated serenity.

Her voice, once bright and curious, had become a hesitant murmur, as though speaking too loudly might trigger disapproval from a world that never stopped watching.

They were all performing.

Every one of them.

And now… Brayden could see it.

The programming.
The masks.
The quiet desperation to be liked. To be accepted. To be enough.

It was everywhere.

And once you saw it, you couldn't unsee it.

He still loved them—fiercely. But it was like watching people he adored acting in a play they didn't know they were in.

Like watching himself, years ago, in reverse.

The veil had lifted.

And somewhere deep within him, something ancient and wordless had already stepped back from the stage.

Just in time.

Because the next scene?

Was about to erupt.

The Unseen Disconnect

Brayden pulled into the driveway, the BMW engine purring into silence. The porch light glowed dimly, casting long shadows across the siding. The house looked still. Too still.

He glanced at the clock on the dashboard.
8:47 p.m.
Again.

A sigh escaped before he could stop it. His hand dragged across his face. *Why do I keep doing this?*

Another evening spent circling, delaying, pretending that space could dissolve what words had left behind. Like maybe silence could solve what speaking had made worse.

He stepped out of the car, the door clicking shut behind him. The walkway felt unusually long. He could feel Mow Ron's nosy stare from across the street, burning into his back like a rash he couldn't scratch.

Inside, the house was quiet—but not the kind that soothes. This was the heavy silence. The kind that follows disappointment. That pools in corners after too many things go unsaid.

He stepped into the foyer. The hardwood met his soles like a splash of guilt.

From the living room came the unmistakable buzz of endless Instagram reels—tiny bursts of laughter and sound rising and falling like waves of synthetic joy. Artificial life looping on a screen.

But it was the kitchen that stopped him cold.

What a mess.

Plates stacked haphazardly in the sink, food crusting at the edges. Crumbs trailed across the counter like evidence of a quiet collapse. A pot on the stove sat congealed and untouched, a glossy skin sealing whatever story had started and then been abandoned. Open cupboards. A red smudge—maybe tomato—streaked across the fridge handle. Used paper towels balled up beside the garbage like tiny white flags of surrender.

No plate waiting for him.

Brayden stood still, heart sinking.

She didn't bother this time.

He tried to shake it off, but the thoughts came anyway—sharp, fast, uninvited.
Is Holly done with me?
Did she finally snap?
Where is she?
How did I mess this up—again?

His shoulders tensed. He rubbed the back of his neck, then turned toward the stairs. *Check on the girls first. Deal with the rest later.*

Upstairs, the hallway buzzed faintly under a dim light. He peeked into Maggie's room.

She was already asleep, curled on her side. Her face looked drawn, colorless. The wastebasket beside her bed overflowed with tissues.

He stepped in gently and brushed a strand of hair back from her forehead. A soft sigh escaped her lips.

I've been so absent, he thought. *Not just physically. I haven't really seen her in weeks.*

Her small frame looked fragile beneath the covers. Like paper under pressure.

He lingered for a moment, then backed out and moved down the hall.

A soft knock. Then Lily's door creaked open.

She sat on her bed next to Precious, knees hugged to her chest. Mascara had bled into faint half-moons beneath her eyes. Tissues were scattered across the floor like snowdrifts after a storm.

"Hey, sweetheart," he said gently. "Everything okay?"

She didn't look up. "Yeah. Just… Maggie wasn't feeling good. I was helping her."

He crouched beside the bed. "You okay?"

She nodded too quickly, wiping at her cheeks with the sleeve of her hoodie. "Just tired."

He didn't push. Lily's emotions were like thin glass—transparent, brittle, easily shattered. She kept them tucked behind silence, behind practiced smiles and whispered *I'm fines.*

He placed a hand gently on her shoulder. "If you ever want to talk… I'm here, okay?"

Another nod. Eyes still locked on the quilt.

He stayed there for a beat longer, then slowly pulled the door closed behind him.

The reels were louder now.

He followed the sound downstairs.

David was sprawled on the couch, phone inches from his face. The screen flickered across his features—blues, greens, reds—like a cheap strobe light. His thumb moved with mechanical precision. Up. Up. Up. A bag of Doritos lay beside him, half-empty, orange dust clinging to his fingers.

Brayden hesitated in the doorway.

Say something? Ask about homework? Comment on the mess?

He opened his mouth—then closed it again.

Instead, he turned toward the kitchen, pulled open the pantry, and grabbed a loaf of bread and a jar of peanut butter.

He spread it slowly, methodically. As if the act itself could anchor him. A quiet ritual of avoidance. An edible distraction.

David didn't move. Didn't look up.

God, how long has he been on that thing?

Brayden could feel the drain coming from the living room. Like the light was being siphoned from his son's body. Like the phone had become the new parent—feeding him noise instead of nourishment.

He bit into the sandwich. The peanut butter clung to the roof of his mouth—dry, bland, uninspired. He chewed and stared out the window.

His designer suit suddenly felt too stiff. Too clean. Too… stupid.

He used to come home to chaos—Maggie and David arguing over who had to set the table, Holly humming in the kitchen, Lily chasing Precious through the hallway.

Now the house felt like a memory foam imprint of what once was.

Family: A Life Remembered.

The Avatar was alive and well here. And he'd helped install the operating system.

He wasn't above it. Not anymore. The late-night drives, the peanut butter sandwiches, the overthinking—they were just costumes too. Softer ones, sure, but still disguises. Still fear in a different shade.

But something deeper had begun to shift.

He didn't want to escape anymore.

He wanted to feel—even if it hurt.

Because the pain was real.

And so was the life waiting behind it.

Chapter 6

Breaking the Spell

The Avatar's Trance

Brayden stood in the kitchen, chewing absently, the taste of peanut butter dull and gluey in his mouth. His eyes drifted toward the living room, where David still lay slumped on the couch, face bathed in the pale glow of his phone screen.

What's going on in his world right now? What's he scrolling past?

His mind wandered.

He thought back to his own teenage years—how invisible he'd often felt, even in a crowded hallway. How hard he'd worked just to seem normal. He'd had video games and music to cope—temporary escapes with clear beginnings and ends. But this? Social media didn't end. It wasn't a break. It was a loop. A bottomless, always-on, never-enough loop.

And David was caught in it.

The more Brayden watched, the clearer it became: his son was drowning in the Avatar's trance—chasing validation, craving likes, measuring his worth through the flicker of strangers' reactions. A trap dressed up as connection. A digital masquerade that left him emptier than ever.

Brayden wiped his hands on a dishtowel and stepped into the living room.

David's thumb moved with practiced rhythm, scrolling for the next dopamine hit. His posture slouched, his expression flat. Eyes darting, unfocused.

"Hey, bud," Brayden said softly.

No response.

He moved closer, gently clearing his throat. "Hey… uh… where's your mom?"

David blinked, slowly surfacing. "She went out with Myriam."

Brayden frowned. "Myriam? On a Tuesday?"

David shrugged. "She was pissed. I dunno. Said she needed to blow off steam."

That hit harder than expected.

She left. She didn't wait. She didn't want to see me.

The guilt flared again—sharp, sudden, familiar. He sank into the armchair across from David, running both hands through his hair. The silence stretched between them like a rubber band—tight, uneasy, full of things left unsaid.

He watched his son.

Really watched him.

The heavy eyelids. The restless flick of his thumb. The flickers of emotion that crossed his face with every swipe, every half-second judgment. Microexpressions shaped by someone else's story.

"What are you looking at?" Brayden asked.

David barely glanced up. "Just stuff."

"Stuff?"

"Instagram. TikTok. You know… stuff."

Brayden nodded slowly. *No, I don't know,* he thought. *Not really.*

He had a LinkedIn account. Checked Facebook sometimes. But it had never hijacked his nervous system the way this thing had taken over David's. For his son, it wasn't an app—it was a mirror. One that only reflected back his not-enoughness.

"You been on that thing all night?"

David sighed, melting deeper into the cushions. "Pretty much. Nothing else to do."

Nothing else to do.

Brayden winced. The words hit deeper than David probably meant.

His eyes drifted around the room—board games gathering dust on the shelf, the guitar leaning untouched in the corner, a deflated basketball slouched by the door.

Relics of the boy David used to be.

The one who used to light up. Who laughed freely. Who didn't second-guess his own joy.

Brayden folded his arms. "You ever think about… not being on it? Even just for a little while?"

David rolled his eyes. "Oh God, not you too. Mom's always going on about screen time. It's what everyone does, Dad. It's not a big deal."

But it was. And they both knew it.

Brayden studied his son's face. There was a dullness there. A flatness that didn't belong on a sixteen-year-old. He saw himself again—years ago—trying to fit into a system that rewarded performance and punished softness. Measured worth in strength. Coolness. Control.

He cleared his throat. "You happy, bud?"

David looked up, startled. "What?"

Brayden shrugged, tried to keep it light. "I mean… really happy?"

David blinked. Looked away. "I don't know," he said quietly.

Brayden felt that land like a stone in his chest.

He wanted to say everything. To explain what he'd been learning. That this emptiness David felt wasn't failure—it was the Avatar's wiring. That self-worth isn't something you earn through filters and follower counts. It's something you *remember*, once the noise dies down.

But not tonight.

Instead, he leaned forward, voice low and warm. "If you ever want to talk about it… about anything… I'm here. I know I haven't been. But I'm trying."

David looked up again, eyes surprised. And for a flicker of a second, something softened. He nodded—barely. But this time, he didn't turn his phone back on.

He just held it in his hands. Staring at the dark screen. His own faint reflection staring back.

Brayden watched him, heart heavy.

The Avatar, he thought. *It starts early.*

And if he didn't do something soon, it would root even deeper—turning habits into reflexes, reflexes into addiction, and the craving for validation into a lifetime of chasing shadows.

Suddenly, the doorbell rang, snapping him out of thought.

If this is Mow Ron being nosy again, I swear I'm going to lose it…

He opened the door—but no one was there.

Only a steaming bucket of KFC resting at the foot of the steps.

"What the…?" Brayden squinted down the street. No headlights. No sign of movement. Just the bucket. Still warm. Still unexplained.

"Ding-Dong-Ditch KFC? Is this some weird joke from Holly? Or Mow Ron trying to make peace?"

He shook his head, baffled. But as he reached down to pick it up, something in him relaxed.

It was absurd. Strange. Almost comforting.

A mystery wrapped in crispy skin.

And somehow, he knew—this greasy little offering would be the fuel he didn't realize he'd need… for the long night ahead.

The System Breach

It was nearly 3:00 a.m.

Brayden sat alone in his office, surrounded by shadows and the soft hum of dormant electronics. No footsteps overhead. No doors closing.

Holly still wasn't home.

He slumped into his chair, elbows on the desk, forehead in his hands. His chest ached—tight and raw, like something sacred had cracked open inside him and left the pieces scattered across the floor.

His eyes lifted to the dusty photo on the wall.

Three little faces grinned back at him. Joyful. Wild. Radiant.

He blinked. Hard.

God… how long has it been since they looked like that?

He could almost hear them again—bare feet pounding through sprinkler-soaked grass, giggles erupting from blanket forts, the squeals of butterfly hunts in the backyard dusk.

And now?

Slumped shoulders. Glowing screens. Eyes that barely met his anymore.

When did the light dim? When did I stop seeing them?

A weight settled in his chest—cold and sharp.

I didn't protect them.

He gripped the armrests of his chair. Tears welled.

Maggie.

Pale. Hollow-eyed. Wrapped in a cocoon of Kleenex and silent shame. Eighteen going on eighty, wound so tightly by perfectionism she could barely breathe. She thought her body was the problem—but Brayden saw it now. It was the pressure. The programming. The Avatar had her in a chokehold, whispering that she had to earn her worth or disappear.

She was unraveling—and no one had told her why.

David.

He wasn't steering his life. He was vanishing from it. Dissolving into an endless scroll of filters and flashing novelties, trading his authenticity for a hit of approval. Brayden had seen it in his eyes—hours lost to an algorithm, not connecting but dissolving.

Pixel by pixel.

The digital world didn't want his truth. It wanted his compliance. His performance. And David—brilliant, creative, beautiful David—was feeding it piece by piece, numbed by the illusion that this was what it meant to belong.

And Lily.

Oh God, Lily.

Shrinking herself before she'd even bloomed. Learning to hide her body before she'd ever danced freely in it. Avoiding her reflection like it might betray her. Arms always crossed. Words always careful. She was learning to disappear… before she ever had a chance to shine.

Brayden pressed his palms to his face.

This isn't just adolescence. This isn't random. This is systemic.

A chill threaded down his spine.

It wasn't chaos.

It was code.

And the more he followed the threads, the more deliberate it all seemed.

Holly too—caught in a prettier trap. Curated routines. Designer bags. Book club charm. Tasteful throw pillows. Filtered smiles. But beneath it? The same ache. The same fear. The same ache for worth dressed up in applause.

His gaze slid to the reflection in the glass of the office door.

And me.

The suits. The house. The golf membership. The orchestrated identity. The flawless life.

I'm not outside the system. I am the system.

He exhaled through clenched teeth. Rage and clarity rose together like a tide he couldn't hold back.

We're all trapped. And no one's telling us.

Teachers didn't see it. Therapists labeled symptoms. Schools worshipped obedience. Society glorified hustle. Everyone kept spinning—rewarding the mask, punishing the truth.

And worst of all?

No one ever asks: What's the point of all this?

No one told the kids. Not in school. Not in culture. Not even at home.

No one explained that they were inside a game—a simulation designed to keep them chasing shadows.

That the goal wasn't to win.

It was to wake up.

To remember.

To unplug.

His hands trembled as he opened his laptop.

A few weeks ago, he'd started writing a satirical poem—something light, something silly about the Player versus the Avatar. He'd even sung it to Precious like a Broadway number. But tonight?

He wasn't in the mood for music.

There was nothing funny about this.

Still, the thread tugged again—and he followed it.

His fingers moved like they were being pulled by something larger than him—urgent, raw, alive. The words came like a storm.

He wrote about the Avatar.

The false self we're trained to become. A mask built from fears and roles, insecurities and comparisons. The voice that says *not enough* no matter how hard you try. The self that learns to chase, to please, to survive—but not to be.

He outlined its tactics: approval addiction, imposter syndrome, perfectionism, collapse, overachieving, hiding, numbing.

Then he wrote about the Player.

The Energy Being. The self beneath the mask. The one who remembers we were always whole. Always free. Always home.

Even here.

He poured out everything he had buried—grief, guilt, rage, tenderness, knowing. Every word felt like a crowbar through the false floor of his life.

He typed until his breath came in gasps and his hands cramped from the force of truth.

When he finally stopped, the room was still.

The soft glow of the screen lit his face.

No one had warned him about the game.

But maybe now… he could begin to trace its code.

And maybe—just maybe—he could figure out how to rewrite it.

The Manifesto

By the time Brayden stopped typing, he had surprised even himself.

What began as an emotional purge had evolved into something sharper—a map. A clear, undeniable blueprint for how the world really worked. Not just the outer world… but his inner one too.

The more he reread it, the more obvious it became.

There weren't just different philosophies or lifestyles.
There were two entirely different realities.

And every human being—every moment of every day—was choosing between them.

One was unconscious. Automatic. The default.
The other required awareness. Courage. A willingness to unplug from the noise and tune in to something deeper.

He spent hours condensing what had poured through him into one clean document. He wasn't polishing it for anyone else. He was writing it to remember. To ground it. To hold himself accountable to what he now knew—not just in theory, but in every cell of his body.

It became a side-by-side breakdown. At the top, he scrawled:

The Avatar vs. The Player
Two radically different realities.
Realization: You're not just playing the game… you're playing from one of two identities.

---

1. The Avatar Way (Unconscious Default)
• Survival mode. Always on alert.
• Identified with the mind.
• Needs to fix, control, or earn love.
• Avoids discomfort. Chases pleasure.
• Feels separate, lacking, and never enough.
• Rooted in fear, judgment, and tension.

2. The Energy Being Way (Awake & Free)

- Sees life as energy—no threat, only flow.
- Uses the mind as a tool, not a master.
- Emotions are energy to be moved, not feared.
- Everything is connected and meaningful.
- The NOW is enough.
- Rooted in presence, trust, and inner wholeness.

It wasn't poetry. It wasn't perfect. But it was true.
And once he wrote it down, he couldn't go back.

But as the adrenaline faded, doubt began to creep in—soft, slithery, familiar.

Are you sure about this?
Is this a breakdown disguised as a breakthrough?
Who do you think you are—writing manifestos in the middle of the night?

His pulse quickened. That old panic returned—like a trapdoor opening beneath his feet.

I need to talk to someone, he thought. *Someone who won't laugh. Someone who'll tell me if I'm actually losing it—or if I'm finally waking up.*

Only one name came to mind.

Jake.

Brayden clicked "New Message" and began to type.

Subject: Am I Losing My Mind?

Hey Jake,

I know this is going to sound absolutely nuts, but you're the only person I can talk to about this right now.

So… I've been diving into some books—*The Energy Codes*, *The Power of Now*…
Yeah. I know.
The same stuff I used to roll my eyes at.

But here's the thing: I think I'm actually starting to get it.
And it's kind of terrifying.

It feels like I'm waking up to two completely different realities. Like I've been living in a dream my whole life and just now started noticing the glitches.

Here's what I've been piecing together:

• I used to feel separate from everything. Now I'm starting to glimpse that everything is connected—just not always in ways we can see.
• I used to believe my thoughts were facts. Now I realize most of them are just patterns. Old programs running on autopilot.
• I used to think I *was* this body and mind. But what if that's just the vehicle—and who we really are is the energy behind it all?
• I used to see problems as setbacks or punishment. Now I wonder if they're actually invitations to wake up.
• I used to chase my worth through doing—through achieving, fixing, proving. Now I'm wondering… what if we're already enough, just by being?
• I used to believe safety came from controlling everything. Now I'm starting to trust that maybe—just maybe—there's a deeper intelligence running the show.

Jake…

It's like the foundation of my life cracked open.
And instead of everything falling apart, something clear is rising through the wreckage.

I've attached a rough document I put together—a kind of cheat sheet for this new perspective.

It's called *Two Perspectives: Avatar vs. Energy Being.*

I know it's a lot. And yeah, maybe it sounds a little unhinged.

But I need you to tell me…

Am I losing my mind?
Or finally seeing the truth beyond it?

Brayden

Two Ways to Play the Game

Before heading to bed, Brayden opened the PDF one last time.

The document pulsed on the screen like a mirror—reflecting not just what he had discovered, but what he had lived without realizing. He scrolled through it slowly, line by line, asking himself a quiet question for each one:

Which side am I really living from?

Not in theory. In practice.
Which thoughts, habits, and ways of being had he unconsciously checked off, day after day?

And if he were to hand this list to someone else—to his kids, to Holly—what would they say?

Would they recognize the Player in him… or only the Avatar he'd spent years perfecting?

He exhaled. Heavy. Clear.
It wasn't polished. It wasn't perfect.
But it was honest.

*Avatar Perspective (Default Programming)

The unconscious, conditioned way of living. Focused on survival, driven by fear, and centered on the external world.

Aspect	Avatar Perspective	Energy Being Perspective
Mindset	Operates from fear, judgment, and control.	Operates from love, trust, and surrender.
Mode of Living	Survival mode—always seeking safety and approval.	Trusts in a bigger plan—life is seen as guided and purposeful.
Source of Happiness	Must fix external circumstances to feel okay.	Happiness is created from within by aligning energy.

Aspect	Avatar Perspective	Energy Being Perspective
Role of the Mind	The mind is the master—thoughts are unquestioned.	The mind is the servant—the heart and intuition lead.
Connection to Others	Sees itself as separate and alone.	Experiences oneness and unity with everything.
Identity	Identifies with thoughts, emotions, and the body.	Recognizes itself as an energy field within a greater consciousness.
Control vs. Surrender	Manipulates events to feel safe.	Surrenders to the flow—trusts life's unfolding.
View of Challenges	Challenges are burdens to endure.	Challenges are growth invitations.
Mindset on Abundance	Scarcity—never enough.	Abundance—everything needed is already here.
Approach to Life	Effort, tension, and conflict are normal.	Life flows—obstacles are meaningful.
Decision Making	Driven by worry and analysis. Likes & Dislikes.	Guided by intuition and body awareness, not just past experiences and conditioning.
Preferences and Comfort	Narrow comfort zones defined by the past.	Open to all experience as part of expansion.
State of Being	Low vibration—anxiety, pride, craving.	High vibration—love, peace, joy, clarity.
Problem Solving	Treats thoughts as truth—overthinks.	Listens to life as teacher—follows deeper guidance.

Aspect	Avatar Perspective	Energy Being Perspective
Flow of Energy	Stagnation, resistance, disease.	Openness, movement, healing.
Victim vs. Creator	Life happens *to* me.	Life happens *for* me.
Focus	Fixated on the outer world.	Rooted in the inner world.
Perspective on Life	Life is chaotic and stressful.	Life is interconnected and meaningful.
Breathing Patterns	Shallow, disconnected from the body.	Deep, conscious, life-connected.
Emotional Regulation	Numbs, avoids, distracts, blames, projects, suppresses, denies.	Feels, processes, lets go.
Heart Space	Closed, self-protective.	Open, trusting, available.
Love and Connection	Searches for love externally.	Knows: *I am Love.*
Sense of Security	Rooted in money, image, approval, material safety.	Rooted in inner peace and truth.
Manifestation Belief	Must hustle and grind.	Aligns with intention and flow.
Health and Well-being	Sees health as physical only.	Understands health as energetic alignment.

Brayden shut the laptop and leaned back in his chair.

The dim glow of the office cast long shadows across the walls. The silence felt unfamiliar now—thin, brittle. He glanced at his phone. Still no message.

Holly still wasn't home.

A dull ache bloomed in his chest as a new kind of awareness rose with it. His eyes drifted toward the hallway.

I'll need to get the kids up in the morning. Pack lunches. Find socks. Force them to eat something. Smile.

And then it hit him.

How rarely he'd done any of that.

How much she had carried, quietly, invisibly.

The dentist appointments. The school forms. The gentle reminders only a mother seemed to remember. The never-ending list she'd never complained about.

It's not that I didn't care… I just never looked.

A weight pressed into him—shame laced with clarity. He could feel the imbalance now, not just in their marriage, but in his own awareness. For so long, he'd been running on default. Efficient. Useful. Accomplished.

But not present.

She's been holding this household together… while I've been holding onto a version of myself that wasn't even real.

He rubbed his eyes, exhausted.

There was nothing more to do tonight—except try to rest. But the word *rest* felt foreign in his body.

He stood slowly, his limbs aching with unprocessed weight, and stepped into the dark hallway.

Somewhere in the quiet, a question stirred inside him:
What else have I missed… while playing the wrong character?

As he moved through the shadows, a strange sensation rose in his chest—part grief, part clarity, part anticipation.

He could suddenly see it: how most people spent their entire lives trapped in the role of the Avatar—chasing love, success, and validation, never realizing those things could never fulfill them the way living as the Player could.

Something was unraveling.
And something else… was just beginning to take shape.

Chapter 7

The System Starts to Crack

Sleep Deprivation

Brayden couldn't sleep.

He lay in the dark, eyes open, body still, mind unraveling. The bed felt too big without Holly. The silence—too sharp. Every creak of the house echoed like a dare.

Anger. Shame. Sadness.

What the hell happened?

He rolled over, punched the pillow, stared at the ceiling. The alarm clock blinked in steady red:

4:11 a.m.

Another hour gone.

Am I losing my mind?

Thoughts spiraled—childhood memories, teenage regrets, career trophies that now felt meaningless. His marriage. His kids. His beliefs. Was any of it real? Or had he just followed the script like everyone else?

He could feel it—the Avatar's fingerprints smeared across every page of his life.
He hadn't just worn the mask… he had become it.

But in this raw, lucid moment—for once—he didn't run.
He didn't scroll. Didn't strategize. Didn't fix.

Instead… he watched.

He noticed how his mind leapt from fear to fear, like a monkey swinging between live wires.
But this time, he didn't follow.
He breathed.

In. Out.

Back to the body.
Back to now.

When anxiety surged, he didn't brace.
When fear whispered *you're weak, you're breaking,* he let the words pass through like clouds.

The bait was familiar. But this time, he didn't bite.

Instead, he turned his focus to gratitude. One breath at a time.

The air in my lungs.
The roof above my head.
The miracle of being awake enough to notice this.

It wasn't comfortable.
But it was real.

And strangely… there was strength in that.
Power in not resisting.
Grace in letting the storm pass through him, rather than becoming the storm itself.

By the time the first thread of light crept under the blinds, he hadn't slept a minute.

But something inside him had softened.

He wasn't rested.
But he was clear.

Not numb. Not angry.
Just… present.

And for once, that was enough.

He rose slowly, stretching his arms overhead. The stiffness in his back reminded him how heavy the night had been. Barefoot, he stepped into the hallway—the cool boards grounding him in the now.

And then—reality met him at the threshold.

Lily stood there, backpack slipping from one shoulder, tears already brimming.

"Why didn't she come home?" she whispered, voice cracked and trembling. "Did something happen?"

Brayden's heart cracked open.

She tried not to cry—wiped her face with her hoodie sleeve, trying, always trying, to be easier for everyone else.

He knelt and gently touched her arm. "She's okay," he said softly, even though he didn't know. "She probably went straight to the clinic. I'll check on her at lunch, alright?"

David was pacing in the kitchen, phone clutched tight. "I'm texting her. This is messed up, Dad. You seriously don't know where she is?"

There was edge in his voice—but underneath it… worry.

Brayden met his eyes. "I wish I did. But we'll figure it out. She'll be alright."

David looked away.

Maggie was curled up on the couch, pale and silent, wrapped in a blanket. Her lips parted to speak, but she only winced—then pointed to her throat.

He crouched beside her.

"You're staying home," he said gently. "And I'll be working from here today."

She gave a faint nod. But her eyes—glassy, dim, exhausted—told him everything she couldn't say.

Brayden stood slowly.

His chest felt tight, like he was holding up the entire house.

I can't give them answers. Not yet.
But I can be here. I can be steady.

So he was.

He moved through the morning quietly—packing lunches, cooking eggs, pouring juice.

Every small task became an offering.
A hand on Lily's back.
A quiet *"Thanks, Dad"* from David as he slung on his bag.
A nod to Maggie as he tucked the blanket a little closer around her shoulders.

And when it came time to dress, he bypassed the usual crisp shirt and blazer.
He reached for jeans and a soft grey sweater.
It wasn't armor.
It was him.
Or at least… the version of him that was finally beginning to wake up.

Lately, he'd been putting less energy into fixing the outer world—and more into shifting the weather inside.
He was stunned by how quickly the sky could clear.
A single thought could anchor him—or unmoor him completely.
And more and more, he was realizing: the world didn't have the power to make him feel anything.
Not without his permission.

He just had to remember—peace was only ever one thought, one breath away.
But choosing it over the storm?
That was still the hardest part.

The Breakdown

With Lily and David off to school and Maggie curled back in bed, Brayden tried calling Holly again.

Still no answer. Not even a text.

He stared at the screen a few extra seconds, like sheer willpower might summon a reply.

Nothing.

He exhaled hard and dropped the phone on the desk.
Then sat down in his office chair, opened his laptop, and tried to anchor into something normal.
Something productive.
Emails. Work. Routine. Anything.

But within seconds, his brain short-circuited.
It was like trying to hold water in his hands—everything just slipped through.

Fear. Guilt. What-ifs.
Loops of shame. Regret about the past. Panic about the future.

His chest constricted.
His heart pounded against his ribs like it was trying to escape.
No peace. No clarity. No control.
That same dread again. That helplessness.

He shot up from the chair.
Maybe Jake had replied.
He grabbed his phone off the shelf.
Still nothing.

A hollow thud of disappointment hit his gut.

Without thinking, his body began pacing—tight, mechanical, frantic.
Back and forth like a malfunctioning robot.
His mind was static.
Overloaded.

All noise, no signal.
A tangled web with no center. No anchor.

He couldn't focus.
Couldn't think.
Couldn't breathe.
His nervous system was caught in a loop, screaming for relief.

And so—he defaulted.
Autopilot kicked in.
Straight to the kitchen.

He was already pressing the brew button on the coffee machine before realizing what he was doing.
Familiar motions. Predictable reward. Something he could control.

He tore open the chocolate croissant bag and devoured one in three bites—no ceremony, no taste.
Just... consumption.

It wasn't hunger.
It was escape.
Numbing.

He stared blankly at the countertop, crumbs scattered like ash.
Then his eyes landed on the calendar pinned to the fridge.

Just over one month.
One month since Jen's bookstore.
One month since the glitch in the simulation.
One month since something cracked open and let the light in.

And here he was—standing in a fluorescent kitchen with chocolate on his fingers and doubt in his soul,
spiraling like it was day one again.

He suddenly felt ridiculous.
Just an hour earlier, he was proud of how present he'd been with the kids.
Now he felt like such a fraud.

The inner critic pounced.
You're pathetic.
You're unraveling.
This is why people don't change.
You were never built for this. You can't even hold it together for an hour.

Then came the self-mockery. Bitter and biting.
"My mind is like a rabid monkey on steroids."
"It's a gong show in here."
"This whole spiritual detour? It's embarrassing."

His throat tightened.

Was any of it real?
The signs? The dragonfly? Craig's song? The timing? The shifts?
Or had he just projected meaning onto chaos—desperate to believe there was something more?

The doubt coiled tighter, until it blurred into one brutal possibility:
Maybe I've made all of this up.

And then… the collapse.
No tears. No theatrics.
Just a quiet, exhausted surrender.

He slid down the fridge, limbs folding in on themselves like paper.
Back against cold metal.
Palms covering his face.
Breath shallow. Hands trembling.
The silence screamed.

"I need help," he whispered, hoarse and hollow.
"Help. I need help. I'm losing it."

The words hung in the air like a plea to no one.

And then—
Thud.

A sharp knock at the patio door.

He startled.
Looked up, wiping his face with the back of his sleeve.

There it was.

A dragonfly.

Big. Still.
Shimmering wings, iridescent in the morning light.
Clinging to the glass like a silent messenger.

Brayden let out a dry, incredulous laugh. "Oh, come on," he muttered aloud. "Seriously? Another sign?"

But something about it stopped him.
A flicker of something ancient stirred in his chest.
Not belief.
Not certainty.

Just... a pause in the storm.

His breath slowed.
His shoulders dropped.

Okay. Breathe.

He didn't know what it meant.
Maybe nothing.
Maybe everything.
But it was enough to get him off the floor.

He stood slowly, bones aching from tension.
Walked to the counter. Picked up the phone.

Maybe it's not too late.
Maybe… there's still a way.

He dialed Jen.

"Open Book! How can I help you?" Her voice was cheerful, grounding.

"Hey Jen. It's Brayden. Just wondering if—well, if they drew the name for the conference tickets."

A pause.

"Oh, Brayden…" Her voice softened. "Yeah. They drew it last week. I would've called if it was you. I'm really sorry."

He let out a hollow chuckle. "No worries. I kind of figured."

Another pause.

"But hey… you've still got the books, right? If it's meant to happen, you'll find your way there. Maybe not the way you expected.
The universe doesn't always give us what we *want,* but it gives us what we *need.*"

He nodded slowly, even though she couldn't see. "Yeah. Maybe," he murmured.
But his voice betrayed the sting.

They said goodbye. He hung up.

And the silence returned.

He stared at the phone for a long time, the dragonfly still faintly visible at the edge of the patio door.

What did I think would happen? That the universe owed me a miracle?

The doubt crept back in, soft and cold like smoke beneath a doorframe.

Maybe this is all just delusion.
Maybe I really am losing my mind.

And yet…

Something in him didn't crumble this time.
Not fully.

Because somewhere beneath the noise,
a feeling stirred—
gentle but clear, like a signal from deep within.

Keep going.

The Call

Brayden dragged himself into the backyard, craving air. Light. Something real.
His legs were heavy. His thoughts heavier.
Shame clung to him like sweat.

He dropped onto the patio bench, head in his hands.
What a fool.
What did he expect—divine intervention? A golden ticket?

He wasn't just exhausted from a sleepless night.
He was soul-tired—from hoping this new way of life might actually stick, only to feel it slipping through his fingers again.

Maybe this energy stuff is just spiritual comfort food, he thought bitterly.
Delusional optimism for people who can't face reality.

His phone buzzed.
He ignored it.
Buzzed again.
Then again.

With a groan, he grabbed it. *Jake.*

He hesitated—thumb hovering.
What if Jake read the email and thinks I've completely lost it?

Then—a whisper.
Pick up.

"...Hey," Brayden muttered.

Jake's voice burst through, bright and electric. "Dude. You're not gonna believe this."

Brayden rubbed his eyes. "What now?"

"I just won two tickets to a Science & Spirituality Conference in Orlando!"

Brayden froze. "Wait—what?"

"No joke," Jake said, laughing. "I entered this draw at a bookstore fundraiser weeks ago. Totally forgot. Finally checked my voicemail this morning—bam. Flights, hotel, passes. The whole deal. I thought it was a scam, but it's legit."

Brayden sat up, heart thudding. "You… won tickets? *To that* conference?"

Jake's voice softened. "Yeah. And after reading your email this morning, I just knew—I'm supposed to take you."

Brayden didn't speak.
His breath caught in his throat.

Jake continued gently.
"You're not crazy, man. What you wrote—it landed. Deep. You're not spiraling. You're waking up."

The protective shell around Brayden's heart cracked.
"You serious?"

"As a hemorrhoid in January," Jake said.

Brayden laughed—more exhale than sound. "Yeah. Yeah, man. I'm in."

Relief washed over him, warm and quiet.
His muscles softened like melting butter.
His breath deepened.

He was still unsure.
Still fragile. Still shaken.
But life had spoken.
And this time…
he was listening.

After hanging up, the tension in his chest finally loosened.
Something inside exhaled.

Life—with all its mess and mystery—had a rhythm.
Not always elegant.
Not always comfortable.
But deeply, unmistakably intelligent.

He stepped barefoot onto the lawn.
The morning air was crisp and fragrant—earth, dew, distant lilac, and yes…
Mow Ron's freshly cut grass.

Something inside ignited.

He felt it.
A spark.
An untameable aliveness.
A pulse connected to everything.

His life—messy, flawed, beautiful—wasn't random.
It was part of something bigger.
Something wild.

And now, in this precious moment,
he wasn't in his head.

He was here.

The laughter came next—pure and sudden.
He dropped onto the back steps and laughed until tears brimmed.
Not because anything was funny…
but because something inside had finally unclenched.

He felt like a boy again—wild with wonder, washed clean in trust.

And then, clear as sunrise:

This wasn't a breakdown.
It was the Avatar in meltdown—its final, desperate gasp before letting go.

The fear. The doubt. The shame spiral—
None of it was truth.

It was the ego's death rattle.
A last-ditch alarm built into the programming—
like an anti-virus, wired to delete anything that threatened the system.

The code had been written for control.
And anything that strayed from the default settings—

anything unfamiliar, uncertain, free—
was designed to feel… wrong.

And now?
He didn't need to fix it.
Didn't need to know what came next.

Because something deeper had taken the wheel.
And that something… could be trusted.

What a shift—to stop seeing life as punishment and start recognizing it as guidance.
Precise. Patient.
Relentless in its devotion to freedom.

He stood, lighter now.
His heart open.
His gaze clear.

Work could wait.

Maggie still needed care—and for once, he wanted to care for her.
Not out of duty.
Out of love.

He entered the kitchen. The wreckage from last night met him like a scene from someone else's life.
Normally, it would've irritated him.
But not today.

Today, he rolled up his sleeves and simply began.

The first dish met warm water.
He paused.
It felt… good.

The tension in his hands eased.
Soap bubbles lifted into the air, catching light like floating rainbows.
He noticed the faucet's hush.
The clink of ceramic.
The breath moving in and out of his body.

No narration. No judgment.
Just presence.

Is this how I lived as a child? he wondered. *Before the noise?*

He smiled.
It was simple.
And rare.

As he scrubbed, he felt the curve of every plate.
The shimmer of each glass.
The temperature of water against his skin.

It was like re-learning how to be alive.

With the kitchen clean, he moved to the stove.
Chopping carrots. Celery.
The knife made smooth, satisfying sounds on the board.

He added garlic and onions to a pot. The scent rose—warm, ancient, comforting.

And then, a thought surfaced:
What if my energy affects the soup?

He didn't dismiss it.

He breathed slowly.
Whispered: "May this bring her healing. May she feel loved."

He stirred with intention.
Every movement sacred.

And as Debussy floated through the speakers, the kitchen transformed.

Steam curled like incense.
Sunlight danced through the window.

This wasn't just cooking.
It was prayer.
Presence.
Peace.

He carried the bowl upstairs and sat beside Maggie as she took her first spoonful.

Her eyes fluttered shut for a moment—like something deeper than hunger had been soothed.
She lit up, surprised. "Dad, where did you buy this? It's fantastic."

Brayden chuckled, a little sheepish. "I made it."

"You… *made* it?"

He nodded.

She slurped again and smiled. "It tastes like love."

His heart cracked open.

He tucked the blanket gently around her and let her rest.

Then, back in the kitchen, he filled a thermos. Sealed it with care.

Every gesture whispered:
I see you. I love you. I'm here now.

With new energy in his step, he grabbed his keys.
Time to visit Holly at the clinic.

What he didn't know…
was just how much she had unraveled in the hours since she left.

The Unraveling

The scent of lavender oil hung in the massage room—soft and familiar.
But Holly barely registered it.

Her hands moved on instinct—pressing, kneading, smoothing fascia and tension—while her own shoulders stayed braced, locked in invisible armor.

He's been so selfish lately. Does he even see it?

Her fingers pressed too hard into her client's shoulders. The woman flinched.
Holly softened her touch, murmured an apology.

I've been holding this whole family together, she thought bitterly. *The meals. The moods. The scheduling chaos. And he's off… reading books? Meditating? Wandering the woods like some monk on sabbatical?*

A dull throb pulsed behind her eyes—a hangover reminder from last night's wine. Too much.
She felt ashamed.
But also… justified.

She'd walked out on the kids. Left them without a word.
Maggie had looked pale. Lily, worried.
But Holly hadn't left to punish anyone.

She'd left to keep herself from exploding.

And now?

She was unraveling.

Her hands kept moving, but her mind hurled worst-case scenarios like grenades.

What if he's lying? What if there's someone else? What if this whole "awakening" thing is just a mask for escape?

She pictured her life falling apart.
Separate homes. Custody schedules.
Quiet explanations over cereal bowls.

Her chest tightened.

When the session ended, she escorted her client out with a soft smile, her voice gentle, practiced. "Take care."

If only I could take my own advice.

As she turned toward her office, the receptionist looked up.
"Oh—your husband's here. He's waiting in the front."

Holly froze.

The air thickened.
Her stomach flipped.

She stepped into the lobby.

There he was.
Brayden. Standing awkwardly.
A bouquet of red roses in one hand. A thermos in the other.
His posture uncertain. His eyes wide open—soft. Present.

"Hey," she said, unreadable. "Let's go outside. I was just about to take my lunch."

They walked around the side of the building in silence, to a small bench beneath a blooming apple tree.
Petals drifted down like confetti—delicate, beautiful, completely at odds with the tension crackling between them.

Brayden sat and turned toward her.

"Holly," he said gently. "I'm sorry. I know I haven't been the most considerate lately. I've been so deep in my own head, I lost sight of how it's been affecting you."

He didn't mention the night before—
the kitchen left in ruins like a silent protest.
Didn't question her.
Didn't scold her for worrying the kids.
Or for disappearing without a word.

He just offered the roses. And the thermos.

"Thanks," she said flatly. "You made soup?"

"For Maggie. She's still at home… not doing great."

She looked up suddenly, eyes sharp and wet.
"Are you cheating on me?"

The question landed like a gut punch—
but Brayden didn't flinch.

Fear surged, as it always had—a reflex.
Heat bloomed in his chest. That old fire, ready to ignite.

He knew the feeling.
Like leaking fuel.
One thought, one spark, and it would all go up in flames.

But this time—
he breathed.

Let the energy move.
Didn't justify.
Didn't defend.
Didn't run.

He inhaled.
Held it.
Exhaled the discomfort.

Felt his feet on the ground.
The breeze brushing his neck.
The soft landing of petals in his lap.

And he stayed.

Holly was getting impatient now.
Part of her was waiting for a reaction.
Bracing for it.

Brayden's silence felt like an eternity.

Finally…
he spoke.

"No, I'm not cheating on you, Holly," he said calmly. "Not in a million years. I love you. I know I've been distant—lost in my own stuff—but I promise you, there's no one else. I'm sorry if you've felt abandoned."

He paused. His breath trembled slightly, but it stayed slow.

"I'm going through something… big. And I've been terrible at explaining it. But I want to do better. I want to show up again. For you. For the kids."

Holly looked at him for a long time.

The question had come from pain, not logic.
And somehow… he hadn't retaliated.
He hadn't shut down.
He had simply stayed.
Present. Grounded. Real.

Her face softened. She buried her nose in the roses and exhaled.

"I'm sorry too. I just… I've been holding it all together for so long, Brayden. I guess I cracked."
Tears slipped down her cheeks.

"I know," he said, reaching gently for her hand. "I see it now. Everything you carry. And I want to do more."

The wind shifted.

Pink petals drifted down like prayers.

Their fingers stayed interlaced.

And in that moment, something shifted.

The weight they'd both been dragging—blame, silence, resentment—lifted.
Not all the way.
But enough.
Enough to make room for breath again.
Enough to feel… possible.

It was like moving from suffocating to weightless.

But would it last?
Would they learn to live from this stillness—
or would the mind pull them back into its noise, its roles, its expectations, its fears?

Neither of them knew.

But for now, beneath the flowering tree,
they simply breathed.

Together.

The Homecoming

Brayden stepped through the front door with no roses in his hands—
but something stronger pulsing in his chest: intention.

Not to fix everything.
Not to make a grand statement.

But to bring warmth back into the space they all called home.

He peeked into Maggie's room first.
She was still asleep, the tension in her face softened, her breath steady.

He lingered in the doorway, a quiet reverence blooming in his chest.
Something unseen had wrapped her in peace.
He whispered his thanks.

Back in the kitchen, he didn't think *What should I make for dinner?*
He thought, *How can I nourish the people I love?*

He rolled up his sleeves—not out of duty,
but as a kind of ceremony.
A subtle act of devotion.

He searched the pantry for something comforting.
A cheesy pasta casserole caught his eye—simple, hearty, nostalgic.
Then, behind the flour, he spotted an unopened brownie mix.

Lily's favorite.

He smiled.
Maybe tonight I can give them more than food.
Maybe I can give them a reason to feel safe again.

Every motion became intentional—not rushed, not mechanical.
When he cleaned the counters, it was like clearing emotional static.
When he preheated the oven, he imagined it warming not just the casserole…
but the whole house.

As he layered pasta and cheese into the baking dish, he silently repeated:
Let this be comfort. Let this be care. Let this be connection.

No candles. No prayer beads.
Just this: presence in motion.

Jazz piano trickled through the speakers as he stirred the brownie mix.
He caught himself humming.
His steps had a rhythm now—not because the challenges were gone,
but because he was framing them differently.

With love instead of fear.

David was the first to appear.
"Whoa," he blinked. "You're… cooking? Is this like, an emergency meal?"

Brayden grinned. "Nope. Just felt like doing something special."

David eyed him skeptically. "And Mom's okay?"

"She is. She'll be home after work."

David nodded slowly. "Good. That's… good."
His gaze drifted to the guitar leaning in the corner.

Brayden gestured. "Wanna play while I finish up? I'd love to hear you."

David hesitated, then picked it up.
A few quiet chords later, music wrapped around them like an old friend.

When the song ended, Brayden clapped.
"That was incredible. Seriously—you've got something."

David shrugged, but smiled. "Thanks, Dad."

Minutes later, Lily burst through the front door, sniffing the air.
"Wait… is that *chocolate*?"

Brayden laughed. "You caught me. And yes—we're doing board game night after dinner."

Her eyes lit up. "No way. You mean it?"

"I do."

Maggie came downstairs slowly, wrapped in a blanket, her voice still hoarse.
"Do I smell… brownies?"

Brayden handed her a glass of water.
"Yup. Glad to see your sinuses are clearing. Dinner's almost ready."

Then the door opened again.

Holly stepped inside—and froze.

The kitchen was clean.
The table was set.
A golden casserole bubbled in the oven.
Brownie batter bowls were neatly stacked in the sink.

And her kids—*her kids*—were smiling.

Brayden crossed the room and kissed her softly, arms wrapping gently around her waist.

David grinned. "Mom, maybe you should hang out with Myriam more often. Turns out Dad's a domestic goddess."

Dinner was warm.
Honest.
Bright.

Between bites, Brayden cleared his throat.
"So… something crazy happened today."

David leaned back. "You made dinner. We've already processed the miracle."

Laughter erupted around the table.

Brayden smiled.
"Jake won tickets to a Science & Spirituality Conference in Orlando. Two tickets. Flights, hotel—the whole deal."

He turned to Holly. "And guess who he invited to go with him?"

Her eyes widened. "You? Wow. Really?"

"Yeah. I know it's sudden, but—"

"It's okay," she said, nodding slowly. "You should go."

Maggie raised an eyebrow. "So… are you joining a cult now?"

Brayden laughed along with the others, though her words landed deeper than they knew.

Still, he let the warmth carry him.

He focused on what was right in front of him—
his beautiful, imperfect family finally feeling like… a family again.

Not healed.
Not fixed.

But opening.

As the last fork scraped the plate and laughter melted into a soft, contented hush,
Brayden leaned back in his chair and let it all wash over him.

The casserole, the brownies, the music, the promise of a board game—
they weren't just moments.

They were medicine.

Something in the fabric of their family had been rewoven tonight.
Thread by thread.
With love and presence.

And yet… beneath it all, something pulsed.
A whisper.

Orlando wouldn't just be a trip.
It would be a turning point.
A doorway into something deeper than anything he'd ever known.

The real journey was about to begin.

Chapter 8

The Player Wakes Up

Prepare for Takeoff

The airport was its usual chaotic symphony—suitcases rumbling like distant thunder, coffee sloshing into cups, announcements echoing overhead like some omniscient narrator trying to herd cats.

But to Brayden, it all felt… different.

He walked beside Jake, weaving through the bustle with surprising calm. The usual airport stress—tight chest, clenched jaw, irrational fear of lost boarding passes—just wasn't there.
Today, everything shimmered with an almost surreal tranquility.
Like the terminal had been dipped in a lighter frequency only he could feel.

They passed a barista aggressively frothing milk while a toddler screamed at full volume about a dropped granola bar.
Brayden should've been tense.
Instead, he found himself smiling.

It was like watching a play: Avatars in motion. Minds in overdrive.
Energy fields—if Dr. Sue Morter was right—buzzing with static from thought spirals, judgments, and unconscious stress loops.
He imagined glowing toroidal fields radiating around each person like cosmic

doughnuts: some bright, some pinched, others flickering with knots and implosions.

He turned to Jake. "You ever feel like you're watching people move through a dream they don't know they're in?"

Jake squinted. "I mean… this is an airport. That's basically the vibe."

Brayden snorted. "Fair."

They arrived at Gate 27 with time to spare. Brayden took a breath and scanned the crowd.
A young couple argued quietly over boarding passes.
An older woman knit furiously beside an emotional support chihuahua.
A businessman shouted into his phone about synergy.

And yet—beneath it all—something beautiful stirred.
He could feel it in his chest: presence.
The stillness beneath the noise.

He hadn't expected clarity in an airport, of all places.
But maybe that was the point.
If he could feel peace here, he could feel it anywhere.

Jake and Brayden sank into padded chairs facing the tarmac, their carry-ons slouched nearby like exhausted travelers.
Brayden shifted his foot—and felt something small roll beneath it. Curious, he reached down and picked it up.

A chess piece.
More specifically, a black king.

He blinked, startled and amused. Out of all the pieces...

He turned it over in his fingers, its weight oddly grounding.
Without a word, he slipped it into his pocket.

It reminded him of those late nights with Craig—the two of them hunched over their battered board, minds locked in silent battle, playing until the world outside faded and the only thing that mattered was the next move.

Eventually, they boarded. Brayden took the window seat.
Jake pulled out his neck pillow and water bottle, bracing himself for the flight.

The plane began its pre-takeoff hum.

Then the intercom crackled.

"Ladies and gentlemen, welcome aboard this Air Canada flight to Orlando," came a calm, cheerful voice.
"My name is Craig, and I'm your In-Charge Flight Attendant today. If you need anything during the flight, please don't hesitate to press your call button. We're here to make sure your journey is safe and comfortable."

Brayden froze.

His eyes widened. His breath caught.

Craig.

He turned to Jake, who was too busy wrestling with his earbuds to notice.

Of all names. Of all days.
He didn't believe in coincidences anymore—but even if he did, this one would be hard to ignore.

The name echoed like a bell in his heart.
Not painful. Just… poignant.

He looked out the window.
The sunlight struck the wing at just the right angle, and for a breathless second, everything shimmered.

He doesn't even know, Brayden thought.
All these years, and I never told him.

Not about Craig.
Not about the accident.
Not about the dragonflies, or the dreams, or the ache that still lingered in his chest like a breath held too long.

It was strange—how something so monumental could remain hidden in a friendship so close.
But the timing had never felt right. Too heavy. Too raw.

Maybe now it would.
Maybe this trip would open that door.

He closed his eyes and smiled, soft and private.

Craig.

Not a wound this time—
but a whisper.

A reminder that this wasn't just a flight.

It was a threshold.

The beginning of a journey far greater than miles.

Soaring

The plane hummed steadily at 30,000 feet, slicing through clouds like a great metal bird.

Brayden sat by the window, Jake beside him.

Below, the world stretched out like a patchwork quilt—rivers like ribbons, forests like swaths of deep green velvet.

Jake leaned back and glanced over. "I gotta say, man. I'm really impressed with this whole… transformation. Never thought I'd see you diving into spiritual books. I always pegged you as Mr. Rational."

Brayden chuckled. "I did too. But once you see the glitch in the code, you can't unsee it."

He gestured out the window. "And all four of the teachers I've been reading—Tolle, Byron Katie, Morter, Singer—they didn't just theorize. They had direct awakenings. Experiences that blew their minds open… and mine too."

Jake stretched his ears and crossed his eyes. "I'm all ears."

Brayden grinned. "You look like a gnome."

Jake smirked. "I prefer *wizard*."

Brayden laughed and continued.

"Eckhart Tolle was on the verge of suicide, thinking, *I can't live with myself anymore.* Then it hit him: *If I can't live with myself… there must be two of me.* And boom—his ego collapsed. He said it felt like falling into a vortex. Woke up in a totally different state of awareness."

Jake raised his eyebrows. "That's insane."

Suddenly, a calm voice broke over the intercom.

"Ladies and gentlemen, this is Craig, your In-Charge Flight Attendant. We'll now be coming through the cabin to offer beverages and a choice of pretzels or cookies. Please have your tray tables down if you'd like to be served."

Brayden froze.

Craig.

His heart skipped.
He didn't look at Jake.
Just breathed.

Trying to refocus, he went on.

"Byron Katie had something similar. Ten years of crushing depression. Couldn't get out of bed. Then one morning, she wakes up on the floor of a rehab center, watching a cockroach crawl across her foot—and suddenly realizes:
without the mind narrating everything, there's no problem. Everything is perfect."

Jake looked dazed. "There really are some strange things happening when we start paying attention."

A few minutes later, Craig appeared with the drink cart.

"Can I offer you something to drink?"

Jake grinned like a mischievous schoolboy. "Is it complimentary?"

Craig blinked. "Uh… yes."

Jake lit up. "Then I'll have a double espresso mocha, extra whipped cream, sprinkle of cinnamon on top."

Craig looked momentarily panicked.

Jake burst out laughing. "Just messing with you, man. Ginger ale's perfect."

Craig chuckled in relief. "Sure thing. And for you, sir?"

Brayden deadpanned, "I'll have a piña colada. No umbrella necessary."

Craig smiled.

"Kidding," Brayden said, grinning. "Ginger ale sounds great."

A few passengers nearby laughed. A woman two rows up smiled.
Someone in the back chimed in, "I was about to ask for a margarita!"

Laughter rippled through the cabin like a breeze—
lifting the mood in subtle but unmistakable ways.

Jake raised his can. "To higher consciousness at high altitude."

Brayden clinked his. "And high vibes at 30,000 feet."

"Speaking of high vibes," Brayden continued, "Dr. Sue Morter had wild energy experiences—seeing fields, getting jolted out of her body, manipulating frequencies. She said it dismantled everything she thought she was."

Jake raised a brow. "An Energy Being, not an Avatar?"

"You got it." Brayden nodded. "Michael Singer too. He was just meditating in the woods when his consciousness expanded beyond his body. He described it as watching thoughts drift by like clouds. Total observer mode."

Just then, Craig's voice returned on the intercom—playfully dry:

"Ladies and gentlemen, we regret to inform you that we are currently out of double espresso mochas with whipped cream and cinnamon… as well as piña coladas. However, we do have soft drinks, tea, coffee, juice, and water. Thank you."

The whole cabin chuckled again.

Jake raised his cup. "We're influencers now."

Brayden laughed. "God help them."

They sipped in silence for a moment.

Then the plane jolted.

Turbulence struck—sharp and sudden.
Drinks rattled.
A few passengers gasped.
Both men grabbed their armrests instinctively.

For a second, it was like the sky cracked open.
A jolt straight into the now.

Brayden's heart pounded.
Jake's eyes darted to his.

And just as quickly… it passed.
Silence returned.

Brayden let out a breath. "Well. There's that."

Jake exhaled. "Talk about getting grounded."

Brayden nodded, leaning back in his seat.

"Anyway… all those authors had one thing in common.
Something shattered their old perception.
And once that happened—
nothing was ever the same.
You can't go back."

Jake was quiet for a beat. Then, simply:

"I'm ready.
To take a higher perspective.
To see what's beyond the matrix."

Brayden turned back to the window.
Sunlight spilled across the wing like gold.

And for a moment, he wasn't just flying.

He was rising.

The New Tribe

When they arrived in Orlando and stepped into the sprawling conference center, Brayden felt an odd but welcome mix of nervous energy and grounded awe.
The air itself felt different here—lighter, like it had been charged with something sacred.

The place was buzzing, but not in the impatient, elbows-out kind of way.
This wasn't an airport.
People moved slowly. Intentionally.
Some gathered in quiet clusters, deep in conversation. Others simply stood still, eyes closed, breathing.

The atmosphere was alive with presence.

Jake nudged him. "So… feel like you found your tribe?"

Brayden scanned the lobby, his shoulders softening.
"Yeah. I don't know how to explain it, but… it feels like home. Like I'm not crazy after all."

They followed signs to the main ballroom, where hundreds of chairs faced a softly lit stage. As they found their seats, the lights dimmed and the room hushed like a reverent tide.

A poised woman walked out under the spotlight—short blonde hair, intelligent eyes, and the kind of calm that made everyone lean in without knowing why.

"Good morning," she said, her voice grounded and warm. "I'm Dr. Jill Bolte Taylor, Harvard-trained neuroanatomist and author of *My Stroke of Insight*."

Brayden perked up. He knew that name.

"In 1996," she continued, "I experienced a massive hemorrhage in the left hemisphere of my brain.
As a neuroscientist, watching my mind dissolve was terrifying—and awe-inspiring. I lost language, logic, and identity.
But what remained… was something more.
I experienced myself as energy. Expansive. Timeless."

A chill ran down Brayden's spine.

"My recovery took eight years," she said. "But the greatest gift was what I discovered: the right hemisphere holds the keys to peace, compassion, and presence.
And the best part? We can choose to access it. Every day."

The crowd erupted into warm applause.

Brayden turned to Jake, eyes wide. "That was… next level."

Jake shook his head, smiling. "Yeah. And somehow, this didn't make it into our high school biology class."

During the break, the hall buzzed again—this time with something richer.
Shared insight. Soft laughter.
The smell of fair-trade coffee and essential oils.

Near a snack table, a silver-haired woman with bright eyes and an Australian accent approached them.

"First time?" she asked warmly.

Brayden nodded. "Yeah. Yours too?"

She smiled. "I lost my daughter four years ago. It cracked me open. At first I thought I was breaking down.
But turns out—I was breaking open."

Brayden's throat caught. "I'm… really sorry."

She nodded gently. "Thank you.
Grief showed me what's real.
I don't want to live asleep anymore."

Without thinking, they hugged—like old friends meeting again after lifetimes apart.

Later, out by a row of food trucks, Jake struck up a conversation with a sharply dressed woman balancing heels and a compostable plate of vegan curry.

"You're far from Wall Street," he joked.

She laughed. "Used to be my playground. Three homes, endless champagne, panic attacks every night."
She gestured to her yoga pants and sun-kissed smile.
"Sold it all. Now I live in Guatemala. I teach yoga and volunteer at orphanages. I've never felt richer."

Jake blinked. "That's one hell of a plot twist."

She winked. "Turns out the real gold was inside me all along."

Back inside, the next speaker stepped onto the stage—tall, calm, golden-haired, elegant.

Her presence was luminous, like she belonged in both this world and somewhere beyond it.

"Healing begins with energy," she said, her voice more vibration than sound.
"Disease doesn't start in the body. It begins in the field.
Shift the energy, and the body follows."

Brayden sat up straighter.

Dr. Sue Morter.

He scribbled notes furiously as she spoke of belief systems as energetic templates—how thoughts and emotions either opened or constricted the energy field.

"Your breath," she said, "is the bridge between your conscious and subconscious.
It's your access point to healing."

Brayden couldn't write fast enough.

"When we struggle," she continued, "it's not because we're flawed.
It's because we're trying to fix pain using the very mechanism that created it—the mind. The Protective Personality."

Brayden circled it:

Avatar = Protective Personality.

Next came Lee Holden, a Qi Gong master who moved with the grace of flowing water. He guided the audience through gentle movements right there in their chairs—softening joints, aligning breath, smiling through the body.

"When you breathe shallowly," he explained, "your energy stagnates.
But when you breathe deeply and gently, you awaken the healing intelligence within."

Brayden followed along.
Soft belly. Open chest.
His tension began to melt.

Then came the scientist from the HeartMath Institute.
He showed graphs and live readings that measured the electromagnetic fields of the human heart.

"Focused breath. Positive emotion. That's the code," he said.
"The heart is the command center of your biofield.
Learn to regulate it, and your whole life changes."

Brayden stared at the screen, stunned.
He already knew this—not with his intellect, but with something older.
Like truth that had been buried in his bones, just waiting to be remembered.

He turned to Jake.
Their eyes met.
No words. Just knowing.

As the final session ended and the crowd filtered out, they remained in their seats.

Jake finally whispered, "That wasn't a conference.
That was… an upgrade."

Brayden exhaled.
His chest was wide open.
His whole body buzzed—like a Tibetan sound bowl ringing with stillness.

Something inside had awakened.
Something vast.

But even in that expansion, a question stirred.
Not fear.
Just a gentle knowing.

Someone—or something—was surfacing.

Leveling Up

After the first full day of the conference, Brayden and Jake found themselves back at the hotel, sprawled in poolside lounge chairs. The Florida air hung thick with humidity, wrapping around them like a towel pulled from a dryer—dense, heavy, oddly comforting.

Overhead, strings of lights cast a golden glow across the courtyard, their reflections waltzing lazily on the rippling pool surface. A live band played mellow jazz beneath a clutch of palm trees, each note drifting upward like smoke and disappearing into the warm night. The air smelled of coconut oil, jasmine, and the faint char of citrus from the poolside grill.

They kicked off their shoes, rolled up their pant legs, and dipped their feet into the glowing water.
It shimmered around their ankles like liquid starlight.

Jake raised a hand to a passing waiter. "We deserve a drink."

Brayden sighed, watching ripples fan out in slow, meditative circles.
"I feel like someone unplugged my entire worldview. Like the foundation cracked, and now I'm just… floating."

Jake grinned. "Welcome to the other side. It only gets weirder from here."

They sat in easy silence—until an unexpected sideshow started splashing up beside them.

A young couple in the pool laughed and flirted… until the guy launched a splash straight into his girlfriend's face.

Her smile vanished.

"Stop, Mike! You know I have my contact lenses in. I don't like being sprayed."

He laughed and splashed again. "Come on, live a little. We're in Orlando!"

She froze.

There was a pause—just long enough for everyone within earshot to brace.

Then she detonated.

"Mike, I've *had it* with you! You selfish imbecile! How many times do I have to tell you things before you take me seriously? I'm *done,* jerk. *See ya.*"

She swam to the edge with impressive speed, hoisted herself out like a Greek goddess of wrath, and stormed off—dripping rage and chlorine in equal measure.

Mike blinked, stunned. "Wait, what just happened?"

Jake turned slowly to Brayden, wide-eyed. "We were just unwillingly subscribed to *Pool Drama Plus.*"

Brayden laughed. "That was harsh. But also… kind of fascinating. People are so easily triggered these days."

Jake nodded. "Honestly, I'd pay extra for the extended version."

Brayden chuckled, then grew thoughtful.
"What he did wasn't great—but that reaction? That didn't come from the splash. That came from somewhere way deeper."

Jake raised an eyebrow. "Straight from the emotional basement."

Just then, their mojitos arrived—frosty glasses rimmed with sugar and packed with crushed mint.

They clinked without a word, the gesture landing somewhere between celebration and surrender.

"To emotional triggers," Jake said. "May life keep showing us where we still have work to do."

Brayden sipped. "And to contact lenses. May they stay dry."

As the sky deepened into indigo and the band softened its tempo, they drifted toward the patio bar and ordered gator bites—Brayden's first foray into Floridian cuisine.

He poked at the golden nuggets with mock suspicion. "You sure this isn't just… fancy pigeon?"

Jake smirked. "Only one way to know."

Brayden took a cautious bite, chewed, then blinked in surprise.
"Okay… not bad. Like if chicken went to CrossFit."

Their laughter melted into the soft clinking of cutlery, murmured conversation, and the occasional splash from the pool.

Brayden felt oddly disarmed—unguarded in a way he hadn't been in years.
Like some inner wall, rusted and heavy, had finally started to give.

Fireworks suddenly erupted on the distant horizon—red, gold, sapphire—bursting in perfect time with the hush that had settled around them.
The sky cracked open in celebration, and palm trees swayed beneath the shimmer like they were clapping in slow motion.

Brayden leaned back in his chair, mesmerized.
He couldn't remember the last time he'd watched fireworks without multitasking—without checking his phone, pretending to listen, or mentally preparing tomorrow's to-do list.
But now… he was just there.
Entirely.
Present.
A kid again.

Then the band shifted.

A new song spilled out across the courtyard—bright, upbeat, unmistakable.

Talking away… I don't know what I'm to say…

Brayden froze.

A-ha. "Take On Me."

Craig's song.

The sound hit him like a blade sheathed in velvet—gentle, but slicing through layers. His shoulders tensed. His jaw locked. His breath caught in his chest. His whole body recoiled.

A flood of memory surged forward:
Craig dancing barefoot in the living room.
Air-drumming with chopsticks.
That crooked smile full of mischief and light.
The way they used to belt out the chorus together like it could save them.

Brayden's hands trembled.
His drink remained untouched.

Across the table, Jake hummed along, nodding with casual recognition—completely unaware.

Something inside Brayden buckled.
A vault door long sealed began to creak.

He could say it.
He could open the door.
Right now.

Tell Jake about Craig.
About the accident.
About the guilt that sat like wet cement in his lungs every time he breathed too deeply.
About the way grief never really left—it just found darker corners to hide in.

But then came the whisper.
The old reflex.

Don't ruin this.
Not now.
Not here.

He stared into the pool, fireworks still blooming in reflection.
His throat ached with unshed truth.
The song played on, each note tightening the knot in his chest.

He didn't speak.
And Jake never noticed.

Brayden told himself: *Maybe tomorrow.*
Maybe when it won't feel so raw.

But a deeper part of him knew—
the moment was already closing.

And if he didn't speak soon,
the silence might win again.

The Unexpected

The next morning, the convention center buzzed like a hive at sunrise—alive with possibility.

The main hallway pulsed with energy as attendees swirled between rooms, sipping kombucha, nibbling fruit cups, scanning schedules, swapping stories, and laughing in warm little clusters.

The scent of incense mingled with herbal tea, and the collective hum of thousands of awakening souls gave the air a charge—like static before a lightning strike.

Brayden and Jake lingered near the central atrium with their smoothies, basking in the vibe.

"Still riding that high?" Jake asked, raising a brow.

Brayden nodded slowly. "Like I got rewired in my sleep."

Then—like a glitch in the simulation—he froze.

Across the hallway, flipping through brochures at the Qi Gong demo table, stood two familiar faces.

Doug and Jasmine.

Colleagues from the engineering firm.

Brayden's stomach did a full backflip.

He looked down fast, gripping his smoothie like a flotation device.
What are they doing here?

The thoughts came in a wave.

What will they think? Am I about to become a meme in the office Slack? What are the odds? Why here? Why now?

The old programming surged to life:

Be afraid. Hide. Play it cool. Be someone they expect.

But this time… something was different.

Brayden *caught the loop.*

That voice wasn't truth—it was the Avatar script. Reflexive. Ancient.
Programmed for survival.

He closed his eyes and dropped into his body. A slow inhale.
A quiet inner whisper.

I feel you. You're allowed to stay.

The fear didn't vanish. But it loosened.

And then—he stepped forward.

"Doug? Jasmine?"

They turned, surprised—and then lit up.

"Brayden?" Doug laughed, eyes wide. "No freaking way! You're here?"

Jasmine beamed. "What are the odds? Never thought we'd see you at something like this!"

Brayden scratched the back of his neck. "Yeah, well… my friend Jake won tickets and dragged me along."

The words spilled out too fast.
And with them came that flicker of old self-abandonment.

Why am I still pretending? Why not just say I wanted to come?

But he didn't shame himself. He just noticed.
No judgment. Just awareness.

Jasmine tilted her head slightly, picking up on the wobble.

But Doug leaned in, eyes bright. "Dude… this stuff changed my life."

Brayden blinked. "Wait—what?"

Doug nodded. "I wouldn't even be here if it weren't for *The Untethered Soul.* A few years ago, I was homeless. Drunk most nights. Totally spiraling. I'd burned every bridge—money, friends, jobs. I was sitting outside a gas station one night, thinking about ending it… when this guy walks by, hands me that book, and just keeps going. Doesn't say a word."

Brayden stared, speechless.

"I almost tossed it," Doug said. "Thought it was new-age fluff. But something in me paused. I opened it—and man… it was like someone reached into my chest and turned on a light."

His voice softened.

"I saw how much noise I was living in. How I believed every thought my mind screamed at me. But that book made me realize—I'm not the voice. I'm the one who hears it."

Brayden's mouth opened slightly.

This was the same Doug who ran design reviews like a Navy SEAL and made flowcharts for snack distribution.

Doug continued. "I got help. Got sober. Started meditating. Everything changed.
Not through effort—through surrender."

Brayden swallowed, his throat tight. "Doug… I had no idea."

Doug smiled gently. "No one does. We all wear masks at the office.
But this?" He gestured around at the flow of peaceful, curious faces.

"This is different. No posturing. No pretending. Just people waking up."

Just then, Jake returned with a smoothie refill, eyebrows raised. "Everything alright?"

Brayden nodded. "More than alright. Jake, this is Doug and Jasmine—colleagues from work."

Jake grinned and extended a hand. "Very nice to meet you. Small world."

Doug shook it. "Smaller every day."

"You guys going to the Michael Singer talk?" Brayden asked.

Doug lit up. "Wouldn't miss it. Hall 4."

Jake raised his cup. "Perfect. Let's go together."

And just like that, they joined the stream—four fellow travelers, side by side.
No masks. No pretense.
Just open hearts and shared momentum.

As the crowd moved around them like a gentle current, Brayden glanced sideways at Doug, his mind quietly spinning.

How many stories like his are hiding in plain sight?

And more importantly…

How many are still waiting to be written—
just waiting for someone to go first?

Chapter 9

Shedding the Old Avatar

The Wizard

The room was packed—every seat taken, people lining the walls, some sitting cross-legged in the aisles—each one clinging to every word Michael Singer spoke.
His calm, measured voice didn't just address the crowd. It moved through them, slicing cleanly through the quiet ache so many carried just beneath the surface.

There was something almost mystical about him—a radiant stillness that rippled through the room like a tuning fork struck in the dark.

Brayden sat between Doug and Jake, hands on his knees, breath steady, alert. There was a hum in the space—not a sound, but a feeling. As if hundreds of people were on the cusp of remembering something ancient and true.

Singer began, voice grounded and clear.

"You think the solution to your problems is out there in the world," he said, eyes sweeping the crowd. "But no one has ever become truly okay by rearranging external things. There's always the next problem."

Doug leaned back, grinning. For him, this was spiritual Disneyworld. He flashed a thumbs-up toward Brayden and Jake, who both nodded. Doug looked again at Brayden. He seemed different—not in appearance, but in energy. Brighter. Less armored. More at ease.

Singer continued, shaping truth with his hands.

"Real transformation begins when you finally admit: *I'm not okay inside.* Not because of the world… but because I've been clinging. To pain. To stories. To fear. That's what's blocking the energy from flowing."

Brayden's breath caught.

He'd spent so much of his life trying to rearrange the furniture of his existence—better job, better routine, better boundaries. More productive hobbies. A cleaner house. A newer car.

He'd chased peace like it was always one self-improvement away.

But the heaviness never left.

Maybe peace wasn't something you *earned* by fixing the outside.
Maybe it was what emerged when you stopped resisting the inside.

Singer paused, letting the silence breathe.

"You made that mess," he said gently, "by holding on to every painful moment you've ever lived through. Every heartbreak. Every rejection. Every fear. You didn't let them go—you stored them. And now they block your energy. That's why you feel stuck."

A woman a few rows up began to cry—not quietly. Her shoulders shook. Her breath stuttered.

Singer offered a quiet nod.
It seemed to whisper: "That's it," he said. "You're doing it. You're letting go."

Brayden's eyes welled.

Could it really be that simple?
Just… stop gripping the pain?

Singer's voice deepened, steady with truth.

"If you're here, it's because you're ready to reclaim your energy—your most precious currency. And you do that by clearing the blockages. Letting it move again. Feeling who you really are beneath the garbage: a powerful, limitless Energy Being."

Brayden scribbled:

- Energy is my most precious currency
- Let it flow
- I am an Energy Being

He felt the room shift—not physically, but energetically.
A shared exhale. A loosening.
An invisible thread tugging each person closer to themselves—and to each other.

Singer softened.
"The mind is a brilliant tool. Use it to build, to solve, to create.
But when you ask it to fix your personal pain?" He shook his head. "That's like asking a blender to file your taxes."

A wave of laughter passed through the crowd. Brayden smiled.

He'd leaned on logic his whole life. Treated the mind like a Swiss Army knife—ready to fix, calculate, control.
But lately… it felt like that crutch was keeping him from walking freely.

Singer leaned in.
"If you want to be free, you have to let go of the garbage. The grudges. The shame. The payoff of being right. The fear.
It's just energy—trapped. Stuck.
It's not who you are. It never was."

Brayden felt something crack. Not painfully—more like a shell giving way to light.

What if the pain was never him?
What if it was just energy… waiting to move?

Singer's final words rang out like a bell, low and luminous:

"How would you like to wake up every morning *genuinely excited* to be alive—not because of what's happening around you, but because something inside

you is finally free? You feel light, open, joyful… no matter what the world is doing.
That's possible.
That's what happens when you stop clinging. To anything.
Let life move through you—and you've found freedom."

Brayden closed his eyes.
His heart beat slow and steady.
But something inside had changed.

Not because the world had shifted.
But because *he* had.

He turned to Jake, Doug, and Jasmine.
Strangers nearby were smiling through tears.

And for once, Brayden wasn't watching from the outside in.

He was here.

And then, as the stillness settled, a memory stirred.

Craig.
The accident. The grief that swallowed everything.
The hollow silence that followed… and the deafening inner noise that never stopped.

He saw it clearly now—how he had locked it all inside. Buried it beneath a lifetime of *I'm fine.* Like stuffing dynamite into a drawer and hoping no one lit a match.

That's what I've done, he thought.
I didn't let it pass through. I let it settle in—and call it home.

But now… it wasn't shame or despair that rose in his chest.

It was ache.
Clean ache.
Honest ache.

The kind that didn't collapse you—
It cracked you open.

Maybe this was how it started.

Not by fixing.
By *feeling*.

And finally…
By letting go.

The Transformation

Brayden hadn't expected the second day of the conference to outshine the first—but something in the air whispered that it just might.

Yesterday had been expansive—even electrifying. The concepts stirred his intellect, cracked open his worldview, and invited him to see life differently. But today felt quieter. Deeper.
This wasn't about *learning* something new—it was about *unbecoming* something old.

He wasn't just absorbing insights.
He was releasing identities.
Shedding skins.

And the heaviness he'd carried for years—decades, really—was finally starting to loosen its grip.

When Eckhart Tolle stepped onto the stage, Brayden barely breathed. The entire room stilled with him. No music. No flashy entrance. Just a soft-footed man in a beige sweater vest, moving with the quiet composure of someone who hadn't rushed in years.

He didn't need to command the space.
He *was* the space.

He sat. Smiled. Waited.
As if time was not something to conquer, but to gently inhabit.

Brayden blinked. This was the very moment he'd pictured back at Jen's bookstore—the one he'd barely dared to hope for. And now, here it was.

Not because he chased it. Not because he forced it.
But because something deeper had allowed it to unfold.

There was something quietly miraculous about that.

Eckhart didn't try to impress. He didn't posture, pitch, or promise. He radiated the kind of presence that only emerges when someone has fully stopped searching.

He simply *was*.

And in that stillness, something in Brayden softened.
A space opened up.
A memory stirred.

He began to remember what it felt like to be whole.

Tolle began in his familiar gentle cadence:

"The primary cause of unhappiness is never the situation, but your thoughts about it.
What looks negative now may simply be space… being created for something new to emerge."

Brayden leaned in, heart steady—

Buzz.

A vibration rattled in his pocket.
His body tensed. A surge of panic climbed his neck.

"I thought I put that stupid thing on airplane mode," he muttered.

He glanced down—just to silence it.
But it was a message from Holly:

"Maggie's fever hasn't broken in five days. I'm bringing her to Emergency."

The words detonated in his chest.

His nervous system flared.
Get up. Do something. Go home. Now.
His chest constricted. His breath vanished.

Images flashed through his mind—Maggie on a gurney. Holly pacing under sterile fluorescent lights. Carrying the burden alone, again.

He was back in that same frozen place—the one from his birthday night, just before the panic attack.

Not here. Not now.

Sweat bloomed on his brow. His hands clenched. His heartbeat pounded like a drumline in his ears.

Though Brayden was physically in the auditorium, his mind had been dragged through a wormhole—back into fear. Back into helplessness.

Ding.

A small bell rang out—Eckhart's gentle cue to return.

Brayden blinked.

The sound reached into him and knocked, lightly, on the door of awareness.

Come back, it said.

He inhaled slowly. Let it out.

His eyes anchored on Eckhart—like a lighthouse in a storm.

"Whenever you find yourself in a difficult situation," Eckhart said, "you always have three options.
One—can you leave the situation?
Two—can you change it?
If not… option three: can you accept it completely, as it is?
Resisting doesn't help. It only creates suffering.
Worry pretends to be necessary… but it serves no real purpose."

Jake leaned in. "You okay, man?"

Brayden nodded faintly, still grounding himself in breath.
The timing of those words—almost too perfect to be coincidence.

By now, he understood the laws of energy. He knew how the old mind loops tried to hijack moments like these.

But another part of him—a deeper part—also knew:
Panicking wouldn't help Maggie.
Even if he flew home on the next plane, a stressed-out version of himself wouldn't guarantee anything.

What *would* help?

Brayden closed his eyes.

Staying open.
Staying still.
Radiating calm.

He remembered: energy is non-local. It transcends time and space.

The most powerful thing he could offer Maggie—and Holly—was not his fear, but his *peace.*
Not a frantic body, but a grounded presence.
Not control… but coherence.

That was the offering.

Not worry.
But *being.*
Not reaction.
But *alignment.*

Brayden placed a hand on his heart—not to perform, but to remember. To anchor. To return.

"Always say *yes* to the present moment," Eckhart continued. "What could be more futile, more insane, than to create inner resistance to what already is? What could be more insane than to oppose life itself, which is now—and always now?

Surrender to what is. Say *yes* to life… and see how life begins working for you, rather than against you."

Brayden exhaled, the words washing through him like a balm.

This was the real work.

Not fixing the moment.
Not escaping it.
But saying *yes* to it.

For the rest of the talk, he stayed with his breath—one inhale at a time. One exhale at a time.
Gently unwinding from the scramble inside.

He had one of the greatest spiritual teachers alive just meters away—modeling the exact state Brayden longed not just to *understand*, but to *embody*.

And then… something shifted.

It wasn't loud.
It wasn't dramatic.
It was a quiet, inner revolution.

With nothing but a clear intention—and the willingness to witness his mind's panic without obeying it—Brayden crossed a threshold.

From fear… into presence.
From collapse… into coherence.

It felt like the heaviness of his entire life was being rewired.
Realigned.

Love, warm and expansive, radiated outward from his chest—not forced, but natural.
Like a long-dammed river finally flowing again.

He visualized it—this loving current—traveling across states, cities, clouds… all the way to Maggie.

In his mind's eye, he saw her resting peacefully. Her fever breaking. Her body softening.

He saw Holly's shoulders relax. Her eyes soften. Her strength return.

It wasn't a fantasy.
It was a *frequency*.
A living signal.

He whispered inwardly:

Thank you, God, for taking care of my beautiful girls.

A tear slipped down his cheek—not from fear, but from relief.
From the staggering intimacy of knowing… he didn't have to do it all alone.

Ding.

The bell chimed again.
Lunch break.

People stirred—stretching, whispering, collecting their things—as the room exhaled.
But Brayden stayed seated a moment longer, letting the silence settle inside him.

Something had shifted.

Not just in his thoughts—
But in his state.

That text from Holly had cracked him wide open.
The old panic had surged.

And yet—he'd breathed himself back to stillness.

Not by fixing.
Not by figuring it out.

Just… by *being*.

When he finally stood, he spotted Jake, Doug, and Jasmine waving near the atrium.

Jake grinned. "How was that for you?"

Brayden let out a breathy laugh, rubbing the back of his neck.
"Honestly? I think I just learned more about how to stay sane—from a quiet German guy in a sweater vest—than in all my years of school combined."

Jake chuckled. "Yup. Took me decades to realize the voice in my head is the most unqualified therapist of all time. Who's hungry?"

"I'm starving," Brayden said. "I feel like I burned five thousand calories just *sitting* through that session. But I've gotta call Holly first—Maggie's at Emergency."

He said it so calmly, his friends couldn't have guessed the storm he'd just weathered.

That was a superpower.
And they were all getting the upgrade.

Old Patterns Upgraded

Jake, Doug, and Jasmine had wandered a few blocks from the buzzing conference center to a cozy little restaurant tucked beneath a canopy of palms. The place radiated laid-back Florida charm—tropical plants in hand-painted pots, mosaic tiles underfoot, a trickling fountain catching the sun just right. Strings of lights swayed overhead like lazy fireflies waiting for dusk.

They slid into their seats like travelers returning from an interdimensional trek. Around them, the hum of conversation danced with words like *heart coherence* and *quantum fields.*

Brayden was still near the entrance, calling Holly. Nearly two hours had passed since her message.

Ring. Ring. Ring.

"Holly?" he said the moment she answered.

Her voice was tired but lighter. "Still in the waiting room with Maggie. But… she's doing better. Her fever dropped a couple degrees about an hour ago. She was even cracking jokes and flirting with a cute doctor."

Brayden smiled, the tension rolling off his shoulders. "That's amazing. Whatever this is, I think it's already shifting. I'm sending you both all the love and healing energy I've got."

"I can feel it," she said. "How's the conference?"

"Absolutely mind-bending," he said. "I'll fill you in when I'm home. Take care of my girls, okay? I love you."

He hung up, heart light. That feeling he'd had during Eckhart's talk—healing, peaceful, real—wasn't just imagination. Something had already changed.

Back at the table, a cheerful waiter bounced over with the confidence of someone who'd already sold three margaritas before noon.

"Afternoon, folks! Can I tempt you with our signature Rainbow Margaritas? They come with a color-changing straw and a tiny umbrella."

Doug laughed. "Tempting, but I don't need booze to numb out anymore. Turns out it's way cheaper—and way more effective—to meditate than to medicate. Just water for me, thanks."

"Iced tea," Jasmine said with a smile.

Jake raised a brow. "Ginger lemonade. Feeling spicy."

"Iced coffee for me," Brayden nodded.

The waiter jotted it down. "Great choices. Want to see menus?"

Doug grinned. "You trust me?"

"No," Jasmine replied.

"Good," Doug said. "Let's split the butter chicken pizza. It's weird. It works."

"Bold move," Jake admitted. "I respect that."

"Make it extra cilantro," Jasmine added.

"Coming right up!" the waiter said, vanishing into the kitchen.

Their drinks arrived like chilled gifts from the refreshment gods. The breeze teased the edges of their napkins. Sunlight spilled through the pergola, sketching warm stripes across their arms.

Brayden's napkin floated to the ground. As he bent to retrieve it, a quiet *"No way…"* escaped his mouth.

Jake leaned over. "Find some good leftovers down there?"

Brayden sat up, holding another chess piece in his hand—this time, a white king.

"No way," Jake echoed. "What are you—summoning a tournament?"

Brayden laughed, explaining how he'd found the black king at the airport. "If this keeps up, I'll have the whole set."

"Weird," Jasmine said. "But… everything has a reason, right?"

Brayden tucked the piece into his pocket, then turned to Doug. "Pardon my curiosity, but I keep thinking about what you said… being homeless, using just to get by. How do you come back from that?"

Doug leaned back, unflinching. "I didn't fight my way out. I surrendered my way through. I stopped running from the pain and let it hit me. All of it. The grief. The shame. The rage. I didn't avoid it—I felt it. It nearly broke me. But it freed me too."

Jasmine's voice softened. "That's… powerful. I think I've spent years smiling, pretending I'm fine. But I've never really faced what's underneath."

Doug nodded. "Most people don't. But pain's like an unwanted tenant—avoid it, and it keeps living rent-free. Sit with it, really feel it… and it moves out."

Brayden sipped his tea slowly, Doug's words settling deep. He thought of all the years he'd spent dodging feelings with distractions—overworking, overthinking, filling every spare moment with busyness.

Maybe the weight he carried wasn't the past itself…
but the effort to keep it buried.

Just then, the waiter returned, balancing a steaming pizza like a trophy.

"Here's the hero of the hour," he announced, setting it down with flair. The smell was divine—spiced tomato, creamy sauce, bubbling cheese, and just enough char on the crust to make it look gourmet.

Doug grabbed a slice. "To emotional digestion and stepping out of our comfort zones."

Jasmine laughed, clinking crusts. "To letting go."

Jake raised his. "To spicy breakthroughs."

Brayden joined in with a grin. "To butter chicken pizza—and clearing old patterns, one bite at a time."

They ate. They laughed. They shared stories, insights, and the occasional *"Oh my God, this is good."*

But beneath the laughter, something deeper was unfolding—presence, release, peace.

And for Brayden, something quiet stirred in his chest.
A knowing.

He wasn't just *learning* how to change.
He *was* changing.

He wasn't who he'd been yesterday.
And something told him…

tomorrow, he'd outgrow even this version of himself.

The Message

After a nourishing lunch, they made their way back toward the conference center, the buzz of anticipation building with every step.

Just before entering the main hall, Brayden excused himself to use the restroom. He splashed cool water on his face, then leaned over the fountain for a sip.

That's when he felt it—that subtle, almost nervous presence at his side. He hadn't noticed the young man standing nearby until he turned.

"Excuse me," the man said, shifting awkwardly. "Sorry to bother you. My name is Tyler Henry."

Brayden blinked. The name didn't mean much.

"I don't usually do this," Tyler added, voice soft but steady. "It's kind of against my code. But I've never encountered anyone so… insistent. Determined. Stubborn."

Brayden tilted his head, wary. "I'm not following."

Tyler gave a small, apologetic smile. "Someone on the other side is pushing hard to get a message through. I won't go further unless you're open to it. But… he's not taking no for an answer."

Brayden's inner defenses flared, but something in Tyler's eyes disarmed him—clear, kind, unassuming.

He nodded. "Okay. What's the message?"

Tyler took a breath. "It's a male, related to you. He's showing me the Twin Towers… but only one is standing. I'm not sure why. And then he says…"

Tyler glanced upward, like he was tuning into something just out of reach. His voice shifted—firmer, more grounded.

He says…"Hey, Brainiac. You're finally getting it…
Checkmate for the black king.
I'm proud of you.
I'm right here.
I love you."

Brayden's whole body froze.

Brainiac.

No one called him that. No one but Craig. Their secret nickname since childhood.

And the black king…?

His breath hitched. His throat tightened.

There was *no possible way* this man could know.

"Thanks," Brayden managed, his voice raw. "I appreciate you saying that."

Tyler nodded, as if he already understood, then melted back into the crowd.

Brayden stood frozen for a moment, his mind spinning.

Was that the sign I've been waiting for?
Was Craig really… still here?

And what did he mean—*checkmate for the black king*?

Was it a message about the ego?
The false self, finally exposed?
The end of the game he'd been unconsciously playing?

Maybe it had never been about winning.

Maybe the whole point was realizing which side of the board he'd been playing from.

The ground beneath him felt different now—less solid, more alive. The veil… thinner.

When he stepped back into the main hall, the air buzzed like a tuning fork.

Suzanne Giesemann stood at center stage, eyes closed, palms relaxed at her sides. Brayden remembered Holly mentioning her—that night the lights had flickered. The Navy Commander turned medium. He hadn't known what to make of it then.

But now?
Now, he was listening.

Suzanne opened her eyes and smiled, her presence instantly calming the room.

"So many ask if it's possible to connect with loved ones who've passed," she said gently. "I'm here to tell you: yes, it is.
They are closer than you think.
The key is frequency.
When you raise yours, you enter a state where you can receive their messages—not with your mind, but with your whole being."

She paused.

"This afternoon, I'll guide you into that state.
We'll quiet the mind. Drop beneath the noise.
And reconnect with the truth that was never lost."

Brayden's heart was still thudding from his encounter with Tyler—but something in Suzanne's voice began to steady him.

"Close your eyes," she whispered.
"Breathe in.
Breathe out.
Let the body settle.
Let the thinking mind dissolve into stillness."

He followed.

"Now… place your awareness not just inside you, but around you.
The space beyond the body.
The field.
Can you feel it?"

He could.
It was subtle—like a living pulse beyond his skin, intelligent and warm. A gentle buzz climbed his spine. His sense of separation blurred.

And then…

A presence.

So familiar, so close, it stole his breath.

Not memory.
Not hope.
Craig.

Not gone.
Not imagined.
Right here.
Around him.
Within him.

Pure love.

Tears welled in Brayden's eyes.

"Just stay," Suzanne whispered.
"Let the field hold you.
Let your heart listen."

Time dissolved.

For the first time in decades, Brayden wasn't seeking.
He wasn't doubting.
He wasn't chasing.

He was just… *home.*

And Craig was there.

When Suzanne's voice returned, it felt like wind through the trees.

"This is your true self.
The rest—the doubt, the mind, the fear—that's just noise.
This… is who you are."

Brayden exhaled.
His shoulders dropped.
Something old and heavy left his body like a departing ghost.

"And when you open your eyes," she said,
"know this: you never have to leave.
The field is always here.
You are always connected."

Brayden opened his eyes.

The world looked different—sharper, clearer, more alive. People sat in stillness. Some wept. Others held hands, stunned into reverence.

Jake sat beside him, wide-eyed, palms open in his lap.

Suzanne stepped away from the mic, her face radiant.

"Thank you for joining me," she said.
"After the break, stay close.
We have a very special guest joining us."

Brayden turned to his friends, heart pounding with something new.

A knowing.

The biggest shift…
was still to come.

The Sage

The conference wrapped up with a surprise announcement—Byron Katie would be closing the event with one final talk.

As the crowd murmured in excitement, Brayden and the others shuffled back to their seats, still reverberating from the intensity of the meditation. His body felt light. His breath easy. A rare hush had settled over his thoughts.

Katie walked onto the stage with a presence that was paradoxical—delicate and powerful all at once. She radiated calm clarity, her smile effortless and knowing, as if she had already seen the end of every struggle by choosing peace every time.

She invited a woman from the audience to join her onstage.

"Are you ready to do The Work, sweetheart?" Katie asked gently. "What did you write on your worksheet?"

The woman hesitated. "I… well, I'm afraid my husband doesn't love me anymore."

Katie nodded with care. "Is it true?"

The woman blinked. "I think so."

Katie tilted her head. "Can you absolutely know that it's true? Take your time. Go deep."

The woman's eyes began to fill. "No… I guess I can't."

Katie smiled with the tenderness of someone who had been there. "And how do you react when you believe the thought 'My husband doesn't love me anymore'?"

Her voice cracked. "I get angry. I shut down. I push him away. I feel alone."

Katie's gaze was soft but piercing. "And who would you be without that thought?"

The woman inhaled deeply, her body visibly softening. "I'd be… at peace. I'd feel free."

Katie turned to the audience, her voice like sunlight on still water.

"That's it. That's the key. When you believe your stressful thoughts, you suffer. But when you question them, they lose their power. They're just stories—not reality."

Brayden felt a tremor move through him, like a current awakening in his spine. Her words sliced through the fog in his mind, revealing something startlingly simple and profound.

If I'm not at peace, I'm the one who has work to do.

It wasn't blame.
It was freedom.

He thought of the beliefs he'd clung to—the fears, the guilt, the old judgments he dragged behind him like invisible chains. The obsessive thoughts about Mow Ron, tangled in revenge and secret jealousy.

What if it was all just a story?

What if peace was only one questioned thought away?

Doug leaned over, voice hushed and reverent. "That was… wow."

Brayden nodded slowly, the words still echoing inside him.

"Yeah. 'If I'm not at peace, I'm the one who has work to do…'"

He repeated it like a mantra sinking into fertile soil.

Katie concluded her talk with grace, thanking the audience with her hands folded at her heart. The room rose to its feet in a standing ovation. Brayden joined them, though his mind was somewhere else—wandering through the labyrinth of beliefs he'd never questioned, slowly dismantling the walls he'd built around his own heart.

He turned to Doug, Jake, and Jasmine, his voice quiet but resolute.

"This… this changes everything."

The conference ended as quickly as it had begun, as though time had been playing by different rules. The halls slowly emptied, but the air remained thick with something sacred.

Brayden and Jake moved through the final moments in a kind of golden haze.

There were hugs—so many hugs.
Laughter through tears.
Lingering smiles.

Pictures snapped, contact info exchanged, promises made to stay in touch… though deep down, they all knew the magic of this gathering couldn't be preserved in a text thread or Zoom call.

They had met people from all over the world—people who had lost children, fortunes, health—and somehow found clarity and joy on the other side of that loss.

People who had, like them, remembered who they really were.

Brayden felt it rising—
that familiar ache.
The quiet resistance in his chest at the thought of leaving behind what felt like his soul family.
But he had been a good student.
He didn't push the feeling away or bury it.
He welcomed it—like a child coming to him for reassurance.
He let the sadness move through him—warm, raw, honest.

Because he understood now:
grief was just another form of love…
expressing itself as longing.

By the time Brayden and Jake returned to their hotel, the sun was low in the sky. They packed in near silence, both of them full—overflowing, really—with something too vast to name.

On the drive to the airport, Brayden stared out the window at the streets of Orlando passing by.

It occurred to him—this was his first time in Florida.

He hadn't seen the theme parks, the beaches, or any of the usual tourist spots. And yet… he had no desire to.

Because now, probably for the first time ever,
he wasn't looking for something outside.

He was being pulled inward.

And the landscape there?
Utterly unfamiliar. Utterly fascinating.

But finally—
he was ready to stop running. He was ready to explore it.

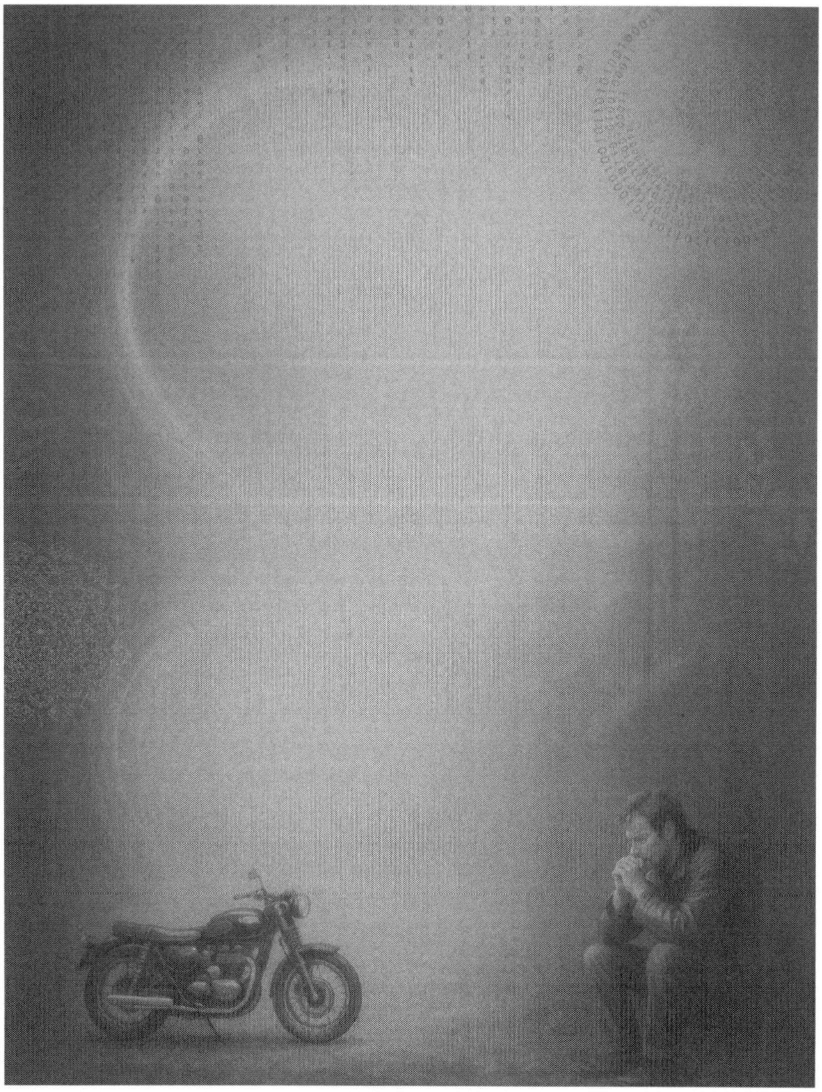

Chapter 10

Reprogramming Reality

Reboot

The plane lifted gently into the clouds, leaving Florida behind as the sun dipped low across the horizon. Inside the cabin, the hum of the engines blended with murmured conversations and the soft ding of the seatbelt sign.

Brayden sat by the window again, watching the sky darken into velvet blue. Beside him, Jake leaned back, a quiet smile on his face.

After a long silence, Jake turned to him. "Man… that was the most empowering experience of my life. No contest."

Brayden nodded slowly. "Same here. It's like… everything's been rewired."

Jake chuckled. "Right? Like we walked through some invisible doorway, and we're not the same people who boarded this flight."

Brayden smiled, then hesitated. A truth rose to the surface—one he had never shared beyond his family.

"There's something I've never told you," he said. "I had a twin brother. His name was Craig."

Jake blinked. "Whoa. I had no idea."

"He died when we were fourteen. A drunk driver hit him. I saw it happen." Brayden's voice cracked. "I carried the guilt for years. I stopped believing in God, in life after death… even in myself."

Jake didn't speak—he just listened, fully.

Brayden pressed a hand to his chest. "But this weekend… something shifted. I know he's still around. Not just in memory. As presence. As energy. I can feel him."

He shared the story of Tyler Henry by the water fountain, the message only Craig could've sent—"Brainiac"—and the black king reference. Then the meditation, where the grief cracked wide open and love flooded in.

"In that moment," he said, "I didn't just remember him. I felt him. Like he wrapped himself around me. It was him. All love. No fear."

Jake's eyes shimmered. "I believe you. My grandmother visited me the night she passed—clear as day. That love doesn't end. It just… shifts form."

They sat in reverent silence.

"I'm not ready to go back," Brayden admitted.

"Neither am I," Jake replied. "But maybe we don't have to go back. Not to the old way."

Brayden looked out at the clouds. "Maybe that's the work now. To show up different."

Jake nodded. "To live like the Player, not the Avatar."

The rest of the flight passed in quiet reflection. No more words were needed. Just presence.

And then—

Home.

Back in his driveway. Back in his bed. Back to the familiar tick of clocks and clink of dishes and low hum of laundry tumbling in the dryer.

Back to the ordinary.

Brayden feared the Orlando magic—far more real than anything conjured by Disney—would vanish the moment he stepped into the gravity of his old life.

But surprisingly… it didn't. Not right away.

The first morning home, he woke feeling more alive than he had in years. The sunlight wasn't just light—it was golden, almost electric. Even the sound of Mow Ron's tractor didn't annoy him.

He kissed Holly with warmth. Sipped coffee slowly. Noticed the steam, the birds, the light in his daughter's hair. He felt—present.

Gratitude came easy. Patience returned. Even the tension at work seemed like background static.

But slowly… it faded.

The next thing he knew, he was slipping into routine… and it all felt strangely surreal. Like Orlando had been a dream he wasn't quite ready to wake up from.

A careless comment from a colleague. A tight deadline. An argument with Maggie over curfew. One by one, the old patterns crept back in. Tension in the shoulders. The compulsion to fix. The need to judge. The Avatar, slipping back on its costume.

Home felt like a different dimension. Orlando had been crystalline—a place where people spoke the language of presence. Here, it was back to buzzing phones, forced smiles, and programmed masks.

And Brayden could see it all now.
Energy blocks disguised as personalities.
Anxiety dressed up as ambition.
Pain pretending to be strength.

Most of all… he saw it in himself.

The pressure to act like "one of the guys" at poker night. The shame of hiding his transformation like a secret. The wasted energy obsessing over Mow Ron's success and swagger.

Despite everything he had learned, the mind still tried to reclaim its throne.
But this time… he noticed.
And that changed everything.

Because once you've seen the code…
you can't unsee it.

And maybe the real work…
was just beginning.

Maybe knowledge was just phase one—and embodiment was the sequel no one warned him would take a decade and several unexpected plot twists.
His habits, conditioning, and programming had taken a lifetime to install. They weren't going to evaporate overnight.

Unfortunately, there was no over-the-counter pill to reset his reflexes or uninstall decades of subconscious beliefs.
Like a stubborn pet, his body had to be retrained. He had to relearn how to breathe—deeply, consciously, deliberately.
Not like he was jogging through life anymore… but snorkeling. Slow, rhythmic, full-bodied breath.

Was he ready to pack up and move out of the penthouse of his mind… and take up residence in the far humbler, messier space of his heart?

He was—because he'd glimpsed what it felt like to live as the Player.
And there was no going back to the prison of the Avatar.

System Overload

Summer vacation had barely begun, and already it was imploding in slow motion.

Holly's little sister was getting married at a vineyard just outside the city—a Pinterest-perfect affair with string lights, handmade flower crowns, and guests who all looked like they belonged in a shampoo commercial.

At least, that was the plan.

The morning of the wedding began with Maggie refusing to leave her room.

"I'm not going," she called from under a weighted blanket and at least three layers of post-pandemic induced germaphobia.

Brayden knocked again. "Mags, we need to leave in twenty minutes."

"I can't! My throat's scratchy, I touched the railing, and there's going to be, like, two hundred people breathing the same air. And the microphone! What if I catch something from the microphone?"

"You'll be fine. Just don't lick it."

Maggie burst into tears. "Dad, I'm serious! I can't do this!"

Meanwhile, downstairs, Lily was dramatically sprawled across the floor in a pink tulle dress, sobbing into a makeup wipe.

"My arms look like raw noodles," she wailed. "And my hair is flat. I'm not going. People are going to take pictures and I'm going to look like a sad toothpick with mascara."

Brayden exhaled through his nose. "Lily, you look beautiful."

"You're my dad. You legally have to say that."

At that exact moment, David emerged from the basement in ripped jeans, a hoodie, and a T-shirt that looked like it had lost a fight with a burrito.

"You're not seriously wearing that," Holly snapped, whirling around in her silk robe and half-done curls, one eye already twitching.

"What? It's clean," David said, sniffing it—and immediately wincing. "Well, mostly."

"Go change. Now."

David sighed like he was being asked to donate a kidney. "Fine."

Twenty-five minutes later, he finally reappeared—this time in ill-fitting khakis and a wrinkled button-up that may or may not have been from sixth grade. He was halfway down the driveway when he suddenly turned around and jogged back inside.

Brayden stuck his head out the car window. "What now? We're already late!"

"Forgot my phone!"

"You don't need your—" But David was already gone.

By the time they arrived at the vineyard, the ceremony had started, Maggie was hyperventilating in the back seat, Lily had re-done her eyeliner five times and now looked like a panda with an existential crisis, and Holly had stopped blinking entirely.

"Okay, okay," Brayden muttered, parking slightly crooked. "Everyone just breathe."

"I can't breathe," Maggie whimpered.

The ceremony was held outdoors under a giant weeping willow, with rows of white chairs and an arch made of purple clematis flowers. It was stunning.

David found a seat near the back and immediately disappeared into his phone. Brayden tried to focus, but he couldn't stop watching David's thumbs dance across the screen like caffeinated caterpillars.

Then it happened.

Right as the couple exchanged vows, a loud TikTok video blared from David's pocket:

"BRO, THIS DOG SAYS 'I LOVE YOU' IN HUMAN WORDS—WAIT FOR IT—"

Heads turned. Holly gasped audibly from the front row. Maggie nearly fainted. The officiant paused. The bride blinked. The groom looked like he was trying to astral project out of his body.

Brayden closed his eyes. "Oh my God."

The woman in front of him whispered to her husband, "That's why kids shouldn't have phones until they're thirty."

Another man muttered, "Disrespectful. Absolutely no awareness. It's a sacred union."

David, oblivious, fumbled to mute his phone—accidentally turning the volume up instead. A dog barked. Someone snorted.

Later, during the reception, Holly cried quietly in a bathroom stall while Lily redid her eyeliner again and Maggie disinfected her glass with a tissue. David stood off to the side, lit by fairy lights, staring blankly at his phone like it was the only thing holding him upright.

Brayden sat alone beneath the willow tree, loosening his tie and watching the stars blink into view.

The game was alive and well. And his whole family was still playing.

By the end of the night, Brayden felt like he'd survived a multiverse collision—one involving teenagers, perfectionism, germaphobia, and a sacred ceremony derailed by a talking dog video. On the outside, he managed to smile for the photos, toast the bride, and dance awkwardly with Lily to a Bruno Mars song she insisted was "vintage."

But inside, his soul felt like it had been sideswiped by a glitter cannon loaded with unresolved family karma.

As they drove home in silence—David on his phone, Maggie curled in the fetal position secretly daydreaming about Samuel, Lily obsessing over her lipstick, and Holly scrolling through wedding photos with quiet, simmering disapproval—Brayden gripped the steering wheel and exhaled, eyes fixed on the road.

He had tasted something real. At the conference. In meditation. In those sacred pauses when the noise fell away and something vast stirred within him. But now, back in the thick of it—suburbia, stress, and sauce-stained khakis—the contrast was almost too much to bear.

It wasn't the first time he'd wondered whether true freedom was possible. But now that he'd *seen* the game for what it was—and understood the rules for exiting—it was no longer a philosophical question.

The stakes were real. The pull, relentless. And the resistance… deeply human.

His intention was clear. His heart, committed. But as the car sped through the dark, a weight pressed down on his chest.

What if the chains ran deeper than he thought—not just into his habits, but into his very sense of self?

He tightened his grip on the wheel.

The thought came, uninvited and sharp:

What if knowing the way out… still isn't enough to leave?

The Tug-of-War

Brayden sipped his coffee before anyone was up, caught once again in the tug-of-war between his new, more mindful routine and the gravitational pull of old habits—like scrolling. Unread emails, half-baked headlines, an ad for gut health gummies, and—randomly—a dating profile still open in a browser tab all felt hollow, but familiar.

The woman described herself as warm, witty, outdoorsy, and emotionally available.
"Looking for someone grounded, emotionally intelligent, and open to growth."
He snorted.
Good luck out there—with all those Avatars.
Then a thought struck him:
What if the Avatar had a dating profile?

He looked at Precious. "It'd probably sound like this…"

TINDER PROFILE: THE AVATAR
Occupation: Overthinker
Interests: Winning arguments, filling silence, avoiding mirrors, staying distracted
Love language: Proving points, passive-aggression, denial, suppression
Philosophy: Seek pleasure, avoid pain
Looking for: Someone to complete me… because I will never be enough.
Age: Timeless (but panicking about aging)
Sex: Sure

Brayden laughed—then shook his head.
If this were an actual profile, he thought, most people would swipe right without realizing *it's them.*

He was getting good at spotting the Avatar in others—but he wasn't free of it himself.

He had underestimated just how tenacious the programming was.
It didn't dissolve in the glow of a conference or spontaneously rewrite itself after a heartfelt meditation.
No.
It crouched in the background—waiting for the smallest opening.

A little while later, Lily wandered into the kitchen.
"Dad, I was wondering… can almond milk give you cancer?"

Brayden, now on his second coffee, was in the middle of an email from his boss titled *Let's talk*—the universal harbinger of doom.

He tried to stay present. Really, he did.

But then Lily pressed, "Dad? Are you even listening?"

And the Avatar pounced.

"I'm trying to get through one email, Lily," he snapped. "Just one."

Her eyes welled up. "I was just asking a question," she whispered.

He sighed. Apologized. Hugged her.
But inside, he knew—it wasn't about almond milk.

It was the damn program.

And if falling into its grip wasn't bad enough, it always circled back to punish him.

Guilt. Shame.
Emotional retribution in surround sound.

It was like a mind virus—quiet, clever, contagious—
weaving a web of reflexes and assumptions that once passed for his personality.

The one who had to get things done.
Stay in control.
Keep everyone afloat.

But now, layer by layer, that identity was cracking.

Interrupting Holly mid-sentence because he'd already finished her thought.
Double-checking David's homework—not out of care, but control.
Clenching his jaw every time Maggie mentioned a new health trend.
The involuntary eye roll when Mow Ron strutted past.

And at work?
It was even worse.

A coworker casually mentioned completing a new training certification.
Brayden nodded, smiled—and immediately felt the sting:

I should've done that. I'm falling behind.

The Avatar loved that game.

It fed on comparison.
Righteousness.
Moral superiority.

It strutted in invisible armor, needing to win arguments, finish sentences, and prove itself in tiny, exhausting ways.

It filled every quiet space with noise—thoughts, podcasts, productivity.
Stillness made it anxious.
Presence made it twitch.

If you boiled it down to one word, it was *insecurity.*

All those needy, neurotic tendencies were just overcompensation for one poisonous belief:

I am not enough.

That belief drove entire lives.

Most never questioned it.

But those who did?
They became Players.
And the game… changed.

One morning at work, during a tense team huddle about retrofit timelines, Brayden could feel the caffeine-fueled tension simmering in the room.

Then Donald—the self-appointed office alpha with the emotional range of a stapler—leaned back, smirking.

"Remind me again why we let engineering near the budget spreadsheet?" he said, loud enough for the whole room to hear.

"Oh right—so we can double our costs *and* finish late."

Silence.

All eyes turned to Brayden.

Doug and Jasmine exchanged wide-eyed looks, eager to see how he'd dodge the bullet.

He didn't flinch.

Just took a slow sip of coffee, locked eyes with Donald, and said:

"Well, someone has to counterbalance accounting's rare gift for combining overconfidence and incompetence."

Boom.
Someone actually *spit out* their muffin like a projectile.
Donald ducked.
Laughter ricocheted around the room.

Brayden gave a calm, deadpan smile and looked back at the agenda like nothing had happened.

But later, alone at his desk, the bitter aftertaste hit.

That little spike of superiority. That sharp jab of self-righteousness.
The cleverness. The cut.

It wasn't connection.

It was performance.
A spike in the system that made the Avatar feel momentarily powerful.

But it came with a cost:
A quiet ache in his chest.
The echo of misalignment.

He stared out the window and whispered to himself:

Damn. That programming.
Sometimes… it just feels so good.

There was a sick kind of pleasure in being right.
In venting.
In feeling wronged, misunderstood, underappreciated, victimized.

It gave him a high.
A hit.
A rush of justification.

But it wasn't *aliveness.*

Not the kind he'd tasted in Orlando.

There, he'd glimpsed something luminous. Spacious. Real.

Here, back in the hum of daily life, that clarity was easy to forget.

Because everywhere he turned, the Avatar was being rewarded.

A snarky text brought a laugh.
A sarcastic jab earned camaraderie or likes.
A judgmental thought passed for insight.

That's when it hit him:

The whole world was basically a five-star hotel for the Avatar—designed to upgrade, feed, and flatter it.

Even the healthy stuff—the gym, his runs, the self-help hacks—could become tools for the Avatar if driven by the same old lie:

I'm not enough yet, but maybe if I do this…

So Brayden stood at a crossroads.
Again and again.
Every day.
A silent tug-of-war.

He had to choose:
The instant gratification of the Avatar…
or the quieter freedom of the Player.

Not easy.
Not sexy.
But real.

Sometimes, he still chose the Avatar—
especially when tired, anxious, or unseen.

But more and more, he paused. He listened.

He whispered his daily mantra:
Do I want to be right, or do I want to be happy?

Even when the honest answer was, *"Hell yeah, I want to be right!"*
That question alone loosened the grip.

One Friday evening at poker night, surrounded by the same old performative masculinity, he felt it.

He couldn't fake it anymore.

The boys weren't ready for the new Brayden.

So he walked away—peacefully.

He was choosing a future no longer ruled by the tyranny of the Avatar.
A future shaped not by fear… but by freedom.

And he was learning to break the chains one…

slow…

link…at a time.

The Bootcamp

Brayden had finally accepted it:
Freedom wasn't a one-time decision.
It was a thousand small ones.
Every single day.

Moment by moment, he had to choose.
Would he keep feeding the Avatar—reactive, righteous, reward-hungry—and collect its fleeting payoffs?
Or live as the Player—rooted, aware, and free?

One path felt familiar. Even a little satisfying.
The other? Uncomfortable. Inconvenient. Uncertain.
But only one led to peace. To real contentment.

Like any skill, that choice required practice. Discipline.
Awareness wasn't a gift—it was a muscle.
And his had grown flabby from years of unconscious living.

So Brayden made a decision:
Time to train.
Not just his mind, but his body too.

Because transformation wasn't just a shift in thinking—
it was a shift in energy.
And energy needed movement.
Flow.
Space.

He laced up his sneakers, headed to the basement, cranked up the music, and started moving.

Not to punish his body.
Not to "get shredded."
But to sweat out the static.
To ground himself.
To shake off the crusty leftovers of stress and stories.

Every breath, every drop of sweat—
it wasn't just exercise.
It was an exorcism.
Of heaviness. Of programming.
Of old identities he didn't need anymore.

Then came the yelling.

At first, he tuned it out.
Weights clinking. Bass thumping.

But those voices—sharp, shrill, undeniable.

Maggie and David.

He paused mid-rep and listened.

"You're so selfish!" Maggie shouted. "You never think about anyone but yourself!"

David fired back, "Yeah? Maybe if you didn't act like everyone's contagious, people wouldn't avoid you!"

"You make me feel crazy!"

"Well, you piss me off! Pardon my French!"

Brayden froze.

There it was—
the whole chain reaction.
Like a slow-motion car crash, but with more hormones.

He could see it now, like a data stream on a screen:

One thought—*He doesn't care about me.*
One chemical flood.
One physical reaction—tight chest, clenched jaw.
One emotional surge—rage.
One behavior—blame.

The Avatar's favorite formula.
And his kids were trapped in it.

He climbed the stairs and knocked on the wall like a human doorbell.
The yelling stopped. Two red faces looked up at him.

"Hey," he said calmly. "I heard some of that. Can I offer something? You're probably not going to love it."

They blinked.

"Nobody can make you feel anything."

David groaned. "Dad, come on… seriously?"

Maggie rolled her eyes. "He literally made me feel like crap."

Brayden nodded. "Not saying it's okay to be unkind. But your feelings don't come from him. They come from what you *believe* about what he said. That's where your power is. Not in blaming. In noticing."

They stared at him like he'd just quoted quantum physics using interpretive dance.

He smiled gently. "Just… sit with it."

And with that, he turned and headed back downstairs.

Would it land? He had no idea.
But the energy had shifted.

Back in the basement, he picked up where he left off.
The body moved. The mind watched.
And the realization deepened.

How had something so basic—noticing a thought—been so foreign for most of his life?

For years, he'd assumed his thoughts were him.
That his reactions were justified.
That he was in control.

But now he could see:

A single thought—*I can't handle this*—could trigger a full biochemical parade.

Tight breath.
Clenched fists.
Heat in the chest.

If the energy moved? It became insight. An experience.
If it didn't? It hardened into emotion.

Anxiety.
Frustration.
Rage.

And all of it?
Started with a thought.
One belief.
That whispered: *This is happening to you.*

Why wasn't this taught in school?
Why were kids memorizing the periodic table, but not learning how to manage the one thing they'd carry their whole lives—their *mind*?

Maybe there was a reason.
Maybe confused, reactive people were easier to control.

The thought hit like a match in dry grass.

Was the game rigged from the start?

His body answered before his mind could:
Shallow breath. Tight jaw. Heat rising like lava.

For a moment, he wanted to punch a wall.
Or a throw pillow.
Maybe both.

But it wasn't about the trigger.
It was about the helplessness underneath.

He saw it clearly now. The contraction. The story.

The belief: *This anger is power. Without it, nothing changes.*

Sneaky.
Seductive.
Familiar.

But another voice—steadier, quieter—rose up:

The anger shows you what matters.
But holding onto it blocks the solution.

He placed a hand on his chest. Took a slow breath.

He didn't suppress the feeling.
Didn't indulge it either.

He let it move.
Like a wave passing through.

And when it did, something else remained:
Peace.
Clarity.
Choice.

From that place, he could respond.
Create.
Lead.

And that was the difference.
Not the force of his fury.
But the strength of his stillness.

The programming still pulled at him. Of course it did.

But strangely, that was a relief.
It meant he had a choice.

Maybe not always in the heat of the moment…
But in the *moments that prepared him for it.*

So he made a plan.
Not a to-do list.
Not a five-year dream map.

A rhythm.
A scaffolding.
A soul bootcamp built around one quiet truth:

The only way out of the Avatar… is through the body.

He committed to daily practices.
Not for ego.
Not to become "spiritually superior."

But to stay *clear*.

- Breathwork to clear the static.
- Qi Gong to keep energy flowing.
- Journaling—not to vent, but to observe.

He called it his *Unmasking Journal*.
Part mirror. Part map. Part quiet rebellion.

Some entries were messy:
- A sharp tone he didn't catch in time.
- A story he believed without checking.
- A judgment that felt true… until it didn't.

Others glowed with quiet wins:
- A pause where there used to be a snap.
- A deep breath instead of a lecture.
- A smile that wasn't forced.

Patterns emerged.

Judgment didn't come from truth—
it came from fear.
Tension followed stressful thoughts.

The body had always known.
It just hadn't been invited to speak.

So he practiced. Day by day.
Not perfectly.
But consistently.

He reached out—to Jake, Doug, Jasmine.
They started weekly check-ins. No ego. No filters.
Just space to tell the truth. To realign.
To remember who they were beneath the noise.

It wasn't flashy.
But it was real.

And in a world that worshipped performance…

real was the most radical thing he could be.

Chapter 11

Multiplayer Mode Unlocked

Real Progress

Brayden kept up his small, consistent habits: taking deeper, more conscious breaths; using tension in his body as a cue to examine stressful thoughts; and keeping his energy flowing with regular movement and time outdoors.

At first, these practices required discipline.
But over time, the rewards—more energy, clarity, peace, and contentment—became self-reinforcing.
It got easier. Natural. Even effortless.

Where he still struggled, though, was coexisting with people who sleepwalked through life in the Avatar's trance—with zero interest in waking up.
The Mow Rons of the world.
That's what triggered him most.
Unfortunately for him, that included most of humanity.
And that's where the real work lived—not on a meditation cushion, but in the messy, noisy trenches of real life.

Sometimes, something as small as opening the fridge and finding an empty almond milk carton could cause spiritual whiplash.

But those moments showed him where the old wiring remained.
So he welcomed them—uncomfortable as they were.
And that was the secret.

Brayden was changing rapidly now. There were many small wins.
He could feel it in his nervous system—in the way his body stayed calm when David shrugged off his chore list, in the way he paused instead of pouncing when Lily stormed upstairs mid-slam.
That was real progress.

But explaining his transformation to three teenagers and a wife who thought his "energy stuff" was just another midlife phase?
That was... tricky.

They weren't reading *The Untethered Soul* or debating the difference between the Avatar and the Player.
They were trying to survive group projects, weird skin breakouts, and the embarrassment of being seen in public with their father.

Still, Brayden saw them now—in ways he never had before.

David, scrolling like it was a survival mechanism—always checking something, refreshing nothing.
"It's how we stay connected," he once said.
But Brayden could feel the quiet desperation beneath it.
The unspoken need to belong.
The Avatar whispering: *You're only as good as your last post.*

If only he could see how magnificently perfect and lovable he already is, Brayden thought.

Maggie, wired tight with invisible tension.
Trying so hard to stay in control that her body was doing the opposite—shutting down.
Her perfectionism wasn't just a personality quirk.
It was a cage.

If only she could stop trying so hard to prove her worth, he reflected, *she might discover that life flows beautifully without planning every second of it.*

And Lily.
Compassionate, funny, painfully self-conscious little Lily.
Fixated on her reflection like she was waiting for the mirror to deliver a verdict.
She checked herself the way some people check their bank balance—hoping for a number that would finally feel like enough.

If only she could see that her body is just a temporary container for the breathtaking being that inhabits it.

He tried to explain what he was learning.
But it was like trying to translate a dream into algebra.

"We're not just our thoughts, Maggie. We're energy. Consciousness. The body is more like… a spacesuit."

She stared at him blankly.
"Dad, has the cult totally brainwashed you?"

Brayden smiled.
"No. But I did unsubscribe from the Matrix."

She smirked and walked off.
"Okay, Morpheus."

It stung—not because she mocked him, but because a small part of him had hoped she'd get it.
That someone—anyone—in the house might say, *Wow, Dad, tell me more about toroidal fields.*

Even Holly, despite her early curiosity, wasn't on board.
She was polite about it—curious, even—but Brayden could feel the distance.

One night, folding laundry side by side, she said gently,
"You're not, like… losing yourself in this stuff, are you?"

Brayden looked up.
"You mean finding myself?"

"I mean," she said carefully, "you've just been kind of… different. Distracted. Philosophical.

I miss just… *us*. Watching movies. Planning vacations. Hosting parties like we used to."

Brayden folded a towel slowly.
"I'm not trying to be different. I'm just trying to be more *me*. My priorities are changing."

Holly sighed, then smiled half-heartedly.

So Brayden backed off.
The books left out "by accident."
The YouTube clips queued up on the family TV account.
The not-so-subtle suggestions.

Instead, he leaned into the practice.
No spotlights. No sermons. Just presence.

He focused on loving them as they were—not as he hoped they'd become.
He reminded himself that the real work wasn't changing other people.
It was staying rooted in truth, even in the middle of their chaos.

Sometimes that meant blessing Maggie's anxiety with patience instead of advice.
Sometimes it meant ignoring David's eye rolls and trusting something was landing beneath the surface.
Sometimes it meant sitting quietly beside Holly as she scrolled real estate listings for places they'd never move to—just to share in the comfort of possibility.

It wasn't flashy.
It wasn't always rewarding.
But it was real.

And Brayden was finally learning:

Real spiritual growth doesn't look like escaping the world.
It looks like staying open-hearted in the middle of a kitchen argument.
It looks like not snapping when the laundry's still sitting in the basket for the third day straight.

It looks like letting your family be exactly who they are—
while quietly becoming who you were always meant to be.

A New World

One year had passed since the dream that cracked his world open.
Brayden's life hadn't become perfect—but it had become something else.
Simpler. Richer. More genuine.

Less like a race, more like a walk through a field where he finally noticed the flowers.

He no longer woke with dread or the compulsion to rant about Mow Ron and check his inbox before brushing his teeth.
Instead, he'd lie in bed a little longer, eyes closed, feeling the quiet hum of life moving through him—subtle, steady, like a current beneath still water.

He was alive—in a way he hadn't known was possible.
Gone were the anxious mornings fueled by ambition and caffeine.
The frantic need to achieve, impress, or *crush the day* had dissolved,
replaced by something quieter.
Something freer.
A childlike enthusiasm.
A gentle curiosity toward whatever called for his attention.

He still worked at the engineering firm—same desk, same projects. But somehow, it all felt different.
Tasks became puzzles instead of problems. Deadlines felt less like doom, more like mild suggestions from time itself.

His coworkers joked, "Nothing rattles Brayden anymore," as if he'd been quietly replaced by a Zen android.
They weren't wrong.

The guy who used to curse at printers and swear in traffic had been replaced by someone who, more than once, paused mid-task just to breathe.

But the shift ran deeper than mindfulness breaks and better sleep.
His entire operating system had changed.

Things that used to dazzle—new cars, luxury dinners, overpriced speakers promising to "elevate your audio experience"—just... didn't anymore.
They were shiny, sure. But they didn't mean much.
It was like decorating a cage and calling it freedom.

Not everyone understood this new version of him.
Holly, especially, struggled to recognize the man who now found more joy in stillness than in champagne toasts or catalog-perfect renovations.

She still lit up for the things they once shared—designer bags, curated events, time-share upgrades.
These gave her sparkle, identity, a sense of control.
And Brayden got it. He really did.
No judgment. Just compassion.

But to Holly, his quiet joy was disorienting.

One afternoon, bags in hand, she turned to him and asked, almost hesitantly, "Don't you want... more?"

Brayden smiled, soft and steady.
"I do have more, sweetheart."

She tilted her head, studying his face like it was a language she used to speak but hadn't heard in a long time.

He understood now.
The Avatar was clever. It wore many disguises—status, comparison, even *treat yourself* culture.
It didn't want peace. It wanted proof.
Applause. Bonus points if you posted about it.

But Brayden had stepped off the hamster wheel—not to renounce life, but to return to it.
To the part that doesn't expire with a trend, or disappear with a paycheck, or fade when the last episode ends.

He had found something deeper.
Something the Avatar could never buy.

Peace.

Not the spa-day kind.
The kind that sits with you in traffic.
That breathes with you while someone's yelling.
That's still there when the dishwasher breaks again and no one loads it properly.

And the most miraculous part?

That peace didn't stop with him.
It began with him—but it rippled outward.
Quietly. Subtly. No announcements. No fireworks.
Just a soft shift in frequency.
A quiet tuning in a loud world.
A silent reordering of what truly matters.

A living invitation:

There's another way to be.
And you'll know you've found it…
when the things you thought you lost
don't feel like losses anymore.

The Test

It started in the driveway.

Holly was digging through the glovebox like it was a lost treasure chest. Maggie was texting Samuel, sighing in rhythmic bursts loud enough to qualify as percussion. David had his earbuds in, bobbing to something vaguely angry. And Lily was already scowling because the car smelled like a pepperoni stick had died under the seat, resurrected, then died again.

Brayden sat quietly in the driver's seat, hands on the wheel, breathing.

Today, it seemed, life had decided to administer a pop quiz.

The moment they pulled onto the main road, a black pickup truck latched onto their bumper like it was trying to merge into their trunk.

"Dad, speed up," David said, lifting one earbud.

"I'm going the limit."

"Well, he's not happy about it," Maggie muttered, glaring into the side mirror.

The truck swerved onto the gravel shoulder, kicked up a cloud of dust, and cut back in front of them with all the grace of a flying trash bin.

Then—poetic justice: a red light.

Now side by side, the driver rolled down his window. Middle-aged. Sunglasses on his forehead. Veins in his neck like angry plumbing.

"You people think you own the road!" he bellowed, gesturing like he was swatting invisible demons. "Wake up, man!"

Brayden turned to him, calm as a monk on melatonin.

"Hope your day gets better," he said, genuinely.

"What the hell does that mean, jerk?"

Brayden smiled. "Just seems like you're carrying a lot. Be well."

The light turned green. The truck peeled out like it had just robbed a gas station.

The car was silent.

Then Lily whispered, "Did you just… bless a road rager?"

"Pretty much," Brayden said, turning left.

"That was either enlightened," Maggie said slowly, "or deeply passive-aggressive. I can't tell."

"I'm gonna try that next time," David mumbled. "Hope your day gets better, bro."

Holly silently shook her head in disbelief.

They reached the grocery store in one emotionally fragmented piece.

The moment they entered—chaos.

A toddler with a full mullet was screaming bloody murder while clinging to a tub of margarine like it was his beloved stuffed animal—until his mom angrily swapped it for a lollipop. Nearby, a man in an Oilers shirt argued with an employee about beef pricing conspiracies. Two elderly women fought over the last watermelon like it was the Holy Grail.

Maggie blinked. "Is it the full moon or something? Mercury retrograde? What's wrong with people?"

"Plenty of Avatars out today," Brayden said, wheeling the cart forward.

As they navigated the aisles, a woman on speakerphone narrated her every thought in real time:

"I came for pasta but now I'm in lost because they moved the damn layout again. I told you about my IBS, right?"

David gagged audibly.

Maggie was ranting to David about microplastics in food when she suddenly froze. Her face turned from pale to beet red. The tomatoes practically camouflaged her.

He laughed—then followed her gaze.

And her reaction made perfect sense.

Over in the dairy section stood Samuel, chatting with his friend Matt.

"Ooooooh! Sexy Sam is here," David said loudly.

"Shut up!" Maggie hissed.

It was incredible how Samuel's presence could scramble her nervous system on contact—dumping a biochemical cocktail of anxiety straight into her bloodstream.

In her mind, *he* made her feel so alive.
But of course, it wasn't Samuel doing it.

It was the chorus of thoughts hijacking her brain:

Oh my god, there he is.
Do I look okay?
Should I go talk to him?
Do I want him to see me with my whole family?
He looks sooooo handsome…

Sweat slid down her brow.

Moments later, Samuel and Matt beelined for the exit, never once glancing in her direction.

Relief and disappointment collided in her chest like waves—crashing, retreating, crashing again.

As she tried to recompose herself, David grinned.

"Aw, Prince Charming left the ball already? He would've loved your tomato complexion."

Maggie ignored him.
She was too focused on the taste of longing. That electric edge of wanting something she couldn't quite define.

She reached for a bag of chips—trying to quiet the ache with salt and vinegar.

Eventually, the family made it to checkout with a full cart and fading patience. Victory was in sight.

Until—

A woman in jogging pants and $800 sunglasses cruised up beside them and parked her cart right in front like she had a FastPass to skip the human experience.

Brayden smiled at her.
"Excuse me—we were just about to move up."

"Oh, I just have a few things," she replied, without eye contact.

Holly bristled. "That's not how lines work."

David cracked his knuckles.

Brayden held up a hand. "Let's not get pulled in."

He felt the tension rise in his belly and took a slow breath, letting it pass through.

Then he looked at the woman—kind, but clear.

"I get it. You're probably in a rush. But we've all been waiting."

She narrowed her eyes. "You don't have to make a big deal out of it."

"I'm not. Just pointing to reality."

Then, like a cosmic wink, a cheery voice called out:

"I can help you over here!"

A second cashier waved them over. Boom—instant line upgrade. No conflict. No cortisol spike.

The family followed, stunned.

As Brayden loaded the bags, Holly stared at him.

"Okay, Gandhi. What's your secret?"

He shrugged. "I just stopped believing that peace comes from controlling other people."

Maggie nodded. "Okay. But if she'd cut me off in traffic *and* at the checkout? I'd probably be in prison."

David fist-bumped him. "Dad, I'm impressed. Like… weirded out, but impressed."

As they exited the store, Brayden held the door for an elderly man who paused, smiled, and said,

"Bless you, young fella."

Then, unexpectedly, the man handed him a small box of chocolates.

"I shouldn't have bought these. I've got diabetes. Your family deserves them."

The kids blinked.

Brayden turned to them, grinning. "See? Karma."

"Or maybe," Lily said, tilting her head, "the universe just gave you a snack-sized reward for not playing the cutthroat game."

Brayden winked. "I'll take it."

And with that, they rolled their groceries into the parking lot like champions of an invisible sport—one where the points weren't for being right,
but for staying present.
Staying calm.
Staying kind.

The Real Influencer

The change didn't stay locked inside Brayden—it began to ripple.
Quietly, but unmistakably, it moved through the heart of his home.
Not because he preached.
Not because he pushed or tried to convince anyone.
But because he *lived* it.

For David—who had spent years measuring his worth by likes and comments—Brayden became a model of quiet confidence.

One Saturday, he invited David on a hike. No agenda. Just movement and air. Halfway up the ridge, shirts damp and breath steady, Brayden paused to take in the view.

"You don't need anyone's approval to know who you are," he said. "You already know. You feel it out here, right?"

David didn't say much. But a few weeks later, Brayden noticed he'd quietly deleted some social apps.
He was playing guitar again.
Taking longer walks.
The need to prove himself had softened.
Something was shifting.

Maggie, still a high achiever with a perfectionist streak, wrestled with anxiety that often showed up as stomach pain before exams.
One evening, as she curled up on the floor in silent distress, Brayden sat beside her.

"Your body's not the enemy," he said gently. "It's talking to you. Let's listen."

He led her through a simple breath practice.
She rolled her eyes—but days later, he saw her sitting cross-legged in her room, headphones on, breathing deeply.
She even asked where she could learn Qi Gong.

And Lily—sweet, unsure Lily—still stared too long in the mirror some mornings.
But they'd started a new nightly ritual.
As he tucked her in, he'd ask:

"What are three things you love about yourself that have nothing to do with how you look?"

Then he'd whisper:
"You are so much more than a body. You are joy. Kindness. Curiosity. That's what we see."

Over time, her gaze softened.
Her smile, once guarded, began to return on its own.

And then there was Holly—his partner in so many seasons of life.
She still carried the weight of years—sometimes numbing with distractions.
But Brayden had stopped offering solutions.
Instead, he just stayed close.
He held space.

"Let it out," he'd say gently. "Don't hide it. Let it move."

Sometimes she cried.
Sometimes she didn't.
But when she did, she always came back to stillness.
And sometimes, when the storm had passed, she would look at him through grateful eyes and whisper, *"Thank you."*

Brayden had become the anchor in a house that used to drift.
Not by force.
Not with wisdom quotes or guided meditations left open on the kitchen counter.
Just by *being*.

He didn't need to fix anyone.
He'd faced his own shadows—and that made him safe in the storms of others.

He wasn't perfect.
But he had discovered how to return to center.
And that alone changed everything.

This—he now understood—was real power.

Brayden's transformation didn't arrive with fireworks or a glow-up montage.
It came more like a gentle exhale after holding his breath for fifty years.
No big announcement. No mystic aura.

Just… space.
Space in his calendar.
Space in his thoughts.
Space between stimulus and response.

He simplified everything—his habits, his reactions, even his relationship with coffee.
And in that simplicity, something wild happened:
He outgrew things that once felt essential.

Conversations that used to ignite him started to feel like reruns.
He no longer needed to prove a point or rescue anyone with his newfound insight.

Whenever he felt off, he remembered his mantra:
"If I'm not at peace, I'm the one who has work to do."

He began questioning what he believed about Mow Ron:
He's a jerk just trying to provoke me.
He saw how believing that made him feel crazy and off-balance.

Slowly, Brayden shifted his thinking:
I can't control others. Only myself. He is who he is—a perfect example of the Avatar stuck in its programming.

His hatred dissolved into compassion.
He no longer called him Mow Ron.
He no longer felt triggered by him.
That was freedom.

Brayden understood now: people were always doing the best they could from the level of consciousness they were at.

Like children who hadn't yet learned better, many Avatars simply lacked the awareness, emotional maturity, or inner tools needed to respond with clarity.

It didn't excuse the behavior—
But it explained the blindness.
And that shift—from judgment to understanding—was everything.

Yes, patience was still required.
But more than that, it called for compassion—for the human condition itself.
So much suffering came not from malice, but from ignorance.
From forgetting who we really are.

He talked less.
Listened more.
Judged almost never.

And in that stillness, people responded—not because he said anything profound, but because they could finally hear *themselves* around him.

Even strangers—Uber drivers, cashiers, old men in line at the hardware store—seemed to open up around him.
He wasn't handing out wisdom.
He was just… there.

A mirror.
Clear. Grounded.
Not there to impress, correct, or fix—just to reflect what was already inside them.

Some people said he'd changed.
Others said he'd gone soft, still believing the programming that kindness is weakness.
One coworker even called him a "push-over."

He didn't mind.
He wasn't trying to be understood anymore.

The strength he'd found wasn't the kind that demanded attention.
It was quiet. Anchored. Undeniable.
And astonishingly powerful.

It moved through the house in ways no lecture ever could.

Maggie's anxiety didn't vanish overnight, but the edge dulled.
There were fewer tears and more conversations.

David still grumbled, but his phone use dipped.
He started playing again.
The guitar came out of the closet.

Lily still had her "I hate everything" mornings.
But once in a while, she'd catch her reflection… and smile.
Just a little.
But sometimes that *little* was everything.

Even Holly—once the queen of curated escape—had started lingering beside him at night.
Just holding a mug.
Just being near.

They didn't talk much.
Sometimes not at all.
But in those moments, the silence said more than any clever turn of phrase.

Brayden didn't need to preach anymore.
He just stayed the course.
Steady. Rooted.
Even when it felt like no one else was walking beside him.

Yes, it was lonely sometimes.
But it was also luminous.

Because he wasn't trying to change them anymore.
He was remembering *himself.*

And somehow, that remembering became a kind of light.
One that didn't need attention.
Just presence.

It didn't trend.
It didn't need to.

Because when you walk in truth—quietly and consistently—
You become the real influencer.

Chapter 12

The Conscious Player

Post-Game Reality

The years didn't pass quietly—
they expanded.

Like rings of energy rippling outward from a single shift in frequency.

Brayden no longer needed to *talk* about transformation.
He had become it.
Not through effort.
Not through striving.
But by living in such a way that his presence alone shifted the room.

He was living proof:
That the game could be seen through.
That the programming could be rewritten.
That when one person remembered who they truly were…
it gave everyone around them permission to remember, too.

And over time, his family began to rise—
not in response to pressure,
but in resonance with possibility.

They were watching him, after all.
They always had been.
And now… they were remembering who *they* were.

Maggie was the first to awaken.

Once riddled with anxiety, perfectionism, fatigue, and illness,
she had lived as a prisoner inside her own skin—
afraid of symptoms, obsessed with control.

But her father's steady transformation cracked the shell.

One night, she asked if she could borrow *The Energy Codes*.
Not with skepticism this time—
but with genuine curiosity.

That was the spark.

She dove in.
Studied breathwork.
Immersed herself in somatic healing, trauma release, and the language of the nervous system.

She didn't just recover—
she thrived.

Her health returned like spring after a brutal winter.
The colds, the chronic exhaustion, the fear of her own body—gone.

By her mid-twenties, she had become a sought-after energy healer.
Her sessions weren't flashy.
But people walked out lighter. Brighter. Stronger.

David took a different route.

For years, he'd been trapped in the feedback loop of the digital world—
scrolling, comparing, refreshing, shrinking.

But Brayden's quiet confidence planted a seed.

One night, David shut his laptop mid-scroll.
Something inside him snapped.

This isn't it, he said aloud.

No one else heard it.
But *he* did.

He started creating instead of consuming.

Launched a YouTube channel—
not to gain followers,
but to question the illusion.

He spoke to teens about identity, awareness, and the trap of the Avatar.
His message was raw, honest, unpolished—
and it spread like wildfire.

Thousands tuned in.
Then millions.

But David didn't care about the numbers anymore.
He cared about the truth.

He was no longer performing.
He was remembering.

He understood:
the earlier teens became aware of the programming,
the easier it would be for them to break free from it.

And Lily—quiet, intuitive Lily—bloomed in her own time.

She had grown up in the shadow of mirrors and metrics,
measuring her worth by waistlines and filters.

But her father's steady love wore down the lie.

Bit by bit, she began to soften.
Speak up.
Laugh more.
Compare less.

What started as quiet journaling turned into weekly circles for girls at her school—

safe spaces where no one needed to perform.
Where tears were sacred, and honesty was power.

The circles grew.
Other schools reached out.
Soon, she was leading workshops across the city—
teaching girls how to reclaim their worth, their bodies, their joy.
How to tap into their intuition and creativity.

She no longer feared her reflection.
Because she knew it was never the whole story.

And Holly… she changed, too.

Not suddenly.
Not in one grand epiphany.

But in subtle, seismic shifts.

The woman who once found control in perfection
began to find power in presence.

Her massage therapy practice evolved.
Clients stopped coming for sore backs
and started coming to be *seen*.
Held.
Understood.

Holly didn't try to fix their pain.
She honored it.
Witnessed it.

And in doing so, created space for miracles.

She never called herself a healer.
But word spread.

And quietly, without fanfare,
she became one.

And then, there was Brayden.

He had long since retired from engineering—
not out of boredom or burnout,
but because life had directed him somewhere else.

He now traveled the world—
not to escape,
but to serve.

Sharing his story—
from living as the Avatar
to embodying the Energy Being he had always been—
had become his life's purpose.

His talks didn't teach as much as ignite.
His presence didn't persuade—
it reminded.

One year, he returned to the Science & Spirituality Conference in Orlando—
not as a student,
but as the keynote speaker.

The same event that had cracked him open years earlier
now welcomed him back as one of its luminaries.

He shared the stage with many of the mentors who had once guided him—
Michael Singer.
Byron Katie.
Eckhart Tolle.
Dr. Sue Morter.
Suzanne Giesemann.

It felt surreal—
and yet, exactly right.

As Brayden stepped onto the stage, the auditorium hushed.

Thousands of eyes lifted toward him—
Jake. Doug. Jasmine…
Holly. Maggie. David. Lily.

Faces glowing in the soft amber light, hearts wide open.

He took a breath.
Not just to calm himself—
but to tune in.

To the moment.
To the energy.
To the collective readiness in the room.

It was electric.

Then he began…

You've Reached the Next Level

Brayden's calm voice resonated through the auditorium.

"Welcome. I'm Brayden Montgomery. About fifteen years ago, at my fiftieth birthday party, I was a total wreck."

A ripple of laughter—uncertain, soft.

"On the outside, everything sparkled. I had a successful career, a beautiful family, a home straight out of a magazine.

But on the inside? I was starving.

Not for more—but for something I couldn't name.

That night, surrounded by candles and laughter and people who loved me, I made a wish.

And I was ashamed of it.

Because I already had so much.

But the wish came anyway, quiet and raw: *I just want to know what's missing.*

Little did I know, that one clear intention—that desperate prayer—would become the spark that reset my entire trajectory.

Not instantly. Not dramatically.

But subtly. Steadily. Irrevocably."

He paused, letting the memory breathe.

"For years, I searched for the missing piece—through achievement, overthinking, and long stretches of numbness. But eventually, I realized:

I'd been asking the wrong question.

It wasn't about what was missing.

It was about what I had forgotten.

I hadn't lost anything. I'd just buried it.

Beneath layers of fear, of programming, of being the good son, the A-student, the strong man, the logical adult—was a magnificent, limitless being of light.

Still intact. Still glowing.

Just waiting for me to remember."

He looked out over the crowd.

"This isn't just my story.

It's *ours.*

We all come into the world radiant—open, free. But childhood teaches us how to survive. We're handed rules. We learn how to behave, how to fit in, how to win the approval of adults who forgot their own light. So we armor up. We hide our magic. We protect ourselves from a world that doesn't feel safe.

And we forget.

But eventually—if we're lucky, and brave—we begin to remember.

Because the truth never leaves us. It only waits.

We knew the way when we were little.

It just wasn't safe to live it back then.

But now? Now we're grown.

Now we can choose."

A stillness spread through the audience like velvet.

Brayden's voice softened.

"There's something I've never shared publicly," he said. "When I was fourteen, I lost my twin brother, Craig. He was hit by a drunk driver while chasing our dog.

I watched it happen."

A collective inhale. The silence deepened.

"For years, I buried it. The guilt. The shame. The feeling that it should've been me. I built a life over that grief, like someone layering wallpaper over a cracked wall. I searched for meaning. I begged for signs. And when none came, I closed the door to hope."

His voice trembled slightly, but he stayed open.

"What I didn't understand… was that Craig never left.

His absence cracked me open so something greater could move through.

That tragedy didn't destroy my life—it dismantled the illusion.

And eventually, when I was ready, it became the doorway to awakening."

He scanned the room. Even the air felt reverent.

"I used to think death was the end. But I've since learned—love doesn't die.

It transforms.

It connects us beyond time and space.

Craig has been with me all along."

He stepped out from behind the podium. His voice deepened, rooted.

"I used to believe I had to earn my worth. That I had to fix myself, control everything, prove something.

But life isn't asking for our control.

It's asking for our trust.

When we stop resisting—when we root into the body and surrender the mind—we return to the truth."

He looked into the audience, steady.

"The truth is—we've been playing a game. All of us. The Avatar game."

Scattered nods passed through the crowd.

"We were born into it. Handed scripts before we could speak. We picked up beliefs, suppressed emotions, wore masks, played roles.

And somewhere along the way… we forgot who we were."

His gaze landed on the front row—Maggie. David. Lily.

"But underneath it all, nothing is lost. Not really.

Who you are—the real you—is not damaged or broken or missing.

You don't need to be fixed.

You need to be remembered."

Silence fell like snow. Thick, luminous, alive.

"When we were children," he said, "we lived in the truth. We played. We loved without fear. We believed in miracles.

That was no accident.

Childhood isn't something we grow out of—it's something we return to.

It's the blueprint."

He smiled gently.

"You're not here to become something new.

You're here to remove the layers. To reboot your system to its original, pristine, optimized state."

The crowd didn't move. They barely breathed.

"Don't hope to feel happy and peaceful next week, or next year, folks. This is it. Right here, right now. This is your life.

If you can't feel content now, you're still stuck in the program—in the game."

"And what's the real goal of the game?" he asked, pausing.

"To wake up from the amnesia. To remember who you are—and why you're here."

He looked up, eyes alight.

"You're here to love. That's it. That's the whole thing. To love each other. Fiercely. Freely. Unconditionally.

Everything else is noise."

Applause began to swell, but Brayden gently lifted a hand—not to stop it, but to anchor them back.

"There's only one way to win the game," he said, voice soft and thunderous all at once.

"Unplug from it. Wake up. Realize you were never the Avatar."

He paused.

"You were the Player all along."

The room held its breath.

Then, without fanfare, the screen behind him flickered to life:

It's Time to Take Back the Controller.
White letters. Black screen. A truth encoded in simplicity.

Then another line appeared:

You've Reached the Next Level.

Brayden looked out at the sea of awakening faces.

Some were crying. Some smiling.

Some standing with hands pressed to their hearts—radiating something deeper than words.

He nodded once, deeply.

And one final message appeared:

Play. Have Fun. But Remember Who You Are.

The ovation rose like a tidal wave. Thunderous. Fierce. Alive.

Suddenly, Craig's song started blasting from the sound system, energizing the crowd even more…

So needless to say
I'm odds and ends
But I'll be stumblin' away
Slowly learnin' that life is okay…

Brayden stood at the center of it all—still, unmoved, completely present.

Not absorbing. Not resisting.

Just being.

The impact of his awakening didn't end on that Orlando stage.

It *began* there.

Because something had been passed on—not a philosophy, not a method, but a living remembrance.

Not because he preached.

Not because he proved.

But because he remembered.

And now—so did they.

Afterword: The Invitation to Awaken

Brayden's journey isn't just his.
It's ours.
It's yours.

Woven from the same threads—fear and love, illusion and truth, forgetting and remembering.

Maybe as you read, you saw glimpses of yourself.
The striving. The self-doubt.
That quiet ache beneath the surface of *"doing fine."*

Maybe you recognized the grip of the Avatar—the voice that measures, protects, performs.

But maybe…

You also felt something else.
Something quieter.
Older.
Truer.

A whisper rising from the stillness:

There is more.
And you've always known it.

It's the reason you've looked at the stars and felt both lost and found.
It's why you've questioned things others blindly accepted.
It's why you're still here—reading, with your heart tilted forward.

You are not broken.
You are not behind.
You are not your story.

You are the one behind the eyes.
The breath behind the thought.
The Player beneath the mask.

You were never meant to stay asleep.

So if something stirred in you—even the tiniest flicker—
Tend to it.
Let it grow.
Let it lead you back to the place you never truly left.

The world will try to pull you back into the performance.
But now… you know the truth.

You've seen behind the curtain.
You've felt what's real.

And now the question is no longer *if* you awaken.
It's this:

Will you live from the one who already has?

Because when you do—
You won't just change your life.
You'll change the game.
For all of us.

Thank you so much for reading!

With love,

Lise Villeneuve

www.consciouslivingsolutions.com

I'd Love to Hear from You!

This book was written from the heart, and I would be truly honored to hear how it impacted yours. Whether something resonated deeply, sparked a shift, or simply made you pause and reflect—I welcome your thoughts.

Feel free to share your feedback, comments, or reviews by contacting me at https://consciouslivingsolutions.com/contact/

Your voice matters! Your insights may help others find their way here.

Special Thanks

With deepest gratitude to the wise and luminous souls whose teachings have profoundly shaped and inspired my journey toward higher consciousness.

Dr. Eben Alexander

Michael Bernard Beckwith

Gregg Braden

Lorna Byrne

Christina von Dreien

Gangaji

Suzanne Giesemann

Thich Nhat Hanh

Dr. David R. Hawkins

Tyler Henry

Lee Holden

Isira

Byron Katie

Nisargadatta Maharaj

Dr. Sue Morter

Mooji

Mary O'Malley

Sister Shivani

Michael Singer

Eckhart Tolle

Estas Tonne

Dr. Jill Bolte Taylor

About the Author

Lise Villeneuve is a Canadian author, wellness educator, and mindfulness mentor devoted to guiding individuals toward self-mastery and a life of joyful flow. With a background in psychology (B.A. Hons., University of Alberta), holistic health coaching, and Reiki mastery, she blends science with spirituality in practical, empowering ways. For decades, she has created, taught, and published mindfulness and emotional literacy programs for people of all ages.

A former international singer-songwriter, Lise's journey led her from the spotlight to a lifelong devotion to conscious living. Her first published work, *Treize Chansons Pour Entendre Son Cœur*, combines a personal development book with an album of original songs, marking the beginning of a lifelong devotion to embodying spiritual truth and awakening others to their innate power through creative expression.

Motherhood deepened that path, inspiring her to create the Conscious Kids Mindfulness Program and later a certification program for educators. She is the author of *Conscious Kids with Wise Willy: Mindfulness & Emotional Superpowers for Families*, a fully illustrated book that helps children and parents explore emotional awareness through powerful stories. She also wrote the transformational novel *Unplugging from the Game: Remembering the Real You*, accompanied by a *Teen Workbook* designed to apply its insights through journaling.

Lise is devoted to using her creativity to help others rediscover the joy, love, and freedom that dwell within.

CONSCIOUSLIVINGSOLUTIONS.COM

Ready To Go Deeper?

Unplugging from the Game is more than a story—it's an invitation to remember who you really are. If Brayden's journey stirred something in you, if you felt the echo of your own questions in his awakening, then the next step is waiting.

The Teen Workbook:

A guided companion to help you unplug, awaken, and take back the controller. Designed especially for teens—but meaningful for anyone ready to live with more awareness and authenticity—this interactive workbook brings the core lessons of the novel to life.

Through each chapter, you'll explore:

- Reflections on identity, emotion, energy, and the mind-body connection
- Self-inquiry questions that help you apply what you've read
- Insights that challenge old programming and limiting beliefs
- Creative prompts to help you reconnect with your true self
- Motivational truths to keep you inspired on the path

Whether you're a teenager navigating the maze for the first time or an adult ready to shed the mask and play from the heart, this workbook is for you. It's not about fixing yourself. It's about remembering who you've always been.

Length: 54 pages. Available at

www.consciouslivingsolutions.com

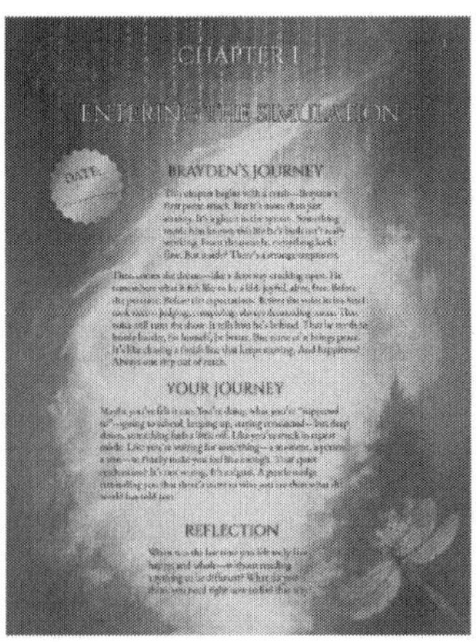

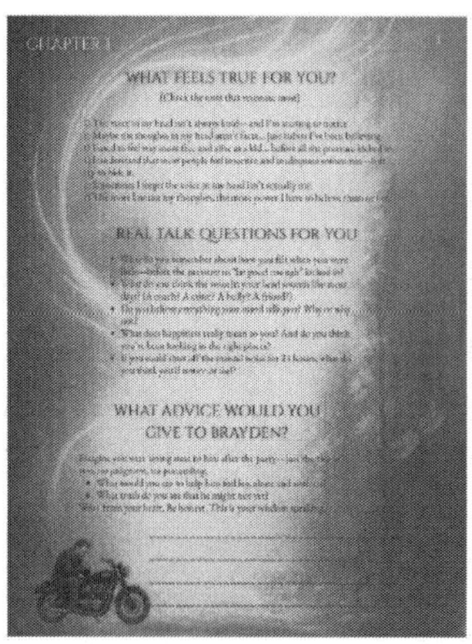

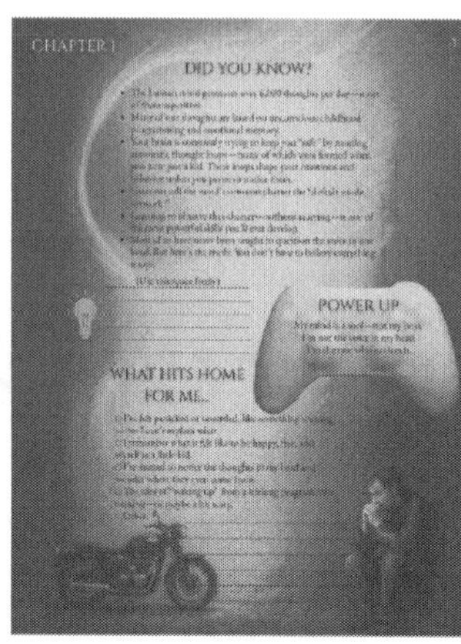

Printed in Dunstable, United Kingdom

70415830R00147